Rooted
In the Infinite

The Yoga of
Alignment

More YOFA™ Resources

www.YOFA.net

www.AffirmativeContemplation.com

www.GreatRelationships.net

www.HealwithYourHands.com

www.VirtualWorkshops.net

www.YOFA.net/blog

Audio,
video, and
interactive resources
for this book can be found at:

www.RootedintheInfinite.com

Rooted
In the Infinite

The Yoga of Alignment

YOFA™ Training
for Spiritual Awareness, Healing,
and Joyful Manifestation

Rebbie Straubing, D.C.

YOFA™
New York

Text, Illustrations, Photographs, and Cover Art

Copyright © 2006 by Rebbie Straubing

The purpose of this book is to help you bring yourself into alignment with your inner truth, and to help you live a happier and more satisfying life experience.

While Rebbie Straubing is trained as a chiropractor and nutritionist, she does not offer health counseling in this book. Her advice is of a general nature meant to assist you in your quest for well-being. She is not a medical doctor or a mental health counselor, and this book is not meant to diagnose, treat, or prevent any medical or psychological condition. This book is not intended to be a substitute for advice from or treatment by a physician, therapist, or other health care professional. If you are in need of medical advice or psychological counseling, you are encouraged to seek the services of a trained professional.

You must exercise your own judgment when using the material presented in this book. The author makes no representations about the suitability of this approach and these exercises for any person or for any specific purpose. This book is provided "as is" without express or implied warranties including, but not limited to, implied warranties of fitness for any particular purpose.

ISBN 978-0-9789065-0-4

*This book is dedicated to
my parents
and to
Danny.*

Contents

Gratitude

It's a bit daunting to aim to acknowledge all the significant influences on this project because I feel I have been working on this book since the day I was born. So, if by chance you don't see your name here and yet you recognize your contribution to my process, I hope you will forgive the brevity of this list and know that you are acknowledged in my heart.

To my mother and father, Alice and Martin Straubing, I am deeply grateful for the all-pervasive lesson of unconditional love. That is what this book is all about. *Mom and Dad, I know you were divinely chosen to teach me this with who you are and I love and cherish my memory of your lives. You live on in between the words of this book.*

To my sister Marsha Straubing, I am deeply grateful for a lifetime of spiritual mentorship. *Marsha, you are my model of a nurturing and compassionate heart. Years and years of your patience and guidance hold the letters together and form the words of this book.*

To my sister Shelli Straubing Abramson, I am deeply grateful for the blazing intensity that profoundly changed my life. *Shelli, you are my teacher. Although it seems I have learned nothing so far, you remain my teacher.*

To my friend and teacher Bernie Weitzman, I am deeply grateful for revealing the inner path so early in my life and in such a profound way. *Bernie, your influence on my life and my work cannot be measured. It probably shows up most noticeably in this book as the sword that edits.*

To my teacher Hilda Charlton, I am profoundly grateful for my awareness of the Divine Presence. *Hilda, you appeared at such a crucial time and in such a potent way, that now, so many decades later, I am inspired to pass along in this book my small stream of understanding of your lessons.*

To Jennifer Lamonica, I am deeply grateful for more than I can focus into words here. *To my soul friend, to you who have saved my life in whatever way one human being can do that for another, many times, our lives are so mingled that I cannot distinguish your specific influence, but I know it is bold and underlined on every page. Thank you for being a model of outrageous, uncompromising, unapologetic spiritual commitment.*

To Daniel Lamonica, I am deeply grateful for a relationship that transcends labels and lifetimes. *Danny, as I aim to pass along to you the stream of unconditional love flowed to me by my parents, I receive the greatest gift of all, the opportunity to love into pure love. You have contributed to the process of this book, year after year, simply by growing up through its evolution. And your deep knowing of the power of words and language, from the time you were born, has provided resonance and instruction for me as a writer. Thank you.*

To Jerry and Esther Hicks and Abraham, I am deeply grateful for bringing into my life, for the first time, a teaching I could whole-heartedly embrace, one hundred percent, with every fiber of my being. *Jerry, Esther, and Abraham, your contribution to the process of this system and this book is in the hum of the words as they are read and made new in the minds of the readers. It is the part that has nothing to do with me, and yet I offer myself in service of that flow. Thank you for including me as an instrument of one small aspect of your message.*

To my friends at *phenomeNEWS*, I offer my sincere appreciation for publishing my articles month after month, year after year. *Thank you for opening an avenue of expression for my work that has allowed it to flow to so many thousands of readers.*

To Sharon Cooper, I am deeply grateful for "unzipping" this book from its quiet little unworded place in my consciousness out into the light of many chapters. *Sharon, without you, this book might only be about seven (unreadable) sentences long. Thank you for your love and patience in extracting and editing my untamed ideas.*

To those who came to me as patients when I was practicing as a chiropractor, to those who have attended my workshops, read my articles, and sent me encouraging emails, *I am deeply grateful for your participation, encouragement, and instruction. I am honored by your willingness to join me on my journeys of exploration through my own healing process—which is really where all my offerings come from. You give me the greatest gift of your friendship as we mingle our journeys in this way. Thank you.*

To Annie Hammond, I am deeply grateful for offering the loving and nurturing space that encourages my expressiveness. *Annie, you bring a sense of peace and an opening into the world that allows this project to flow forward. Thank you.*

Special thanks to Dr. Swami Shankardev Saraswati for so generously sharing his expertise to ensure the accuracy of the chapter on the chakras, to literary agent Sterling Lord for believing in this book from the outset, and to Lindy Cacioppo for her openness, enthusiasm, many commas, and much more.

To my friend and companion Law of Attraction, I am deeply grateful for consistently bringing me a reflection of myself in undiluted, uncensored clarity.

To Divine Love, I am deeply grateful for the flow of ever-present, incomprehensible goodness and for guiding my work.

A Note From Rebbie

S ome teachers can truly be called Masters. They teach from their accomplishment. They exemplify the words *enlightenment*, *guru*, and *mastery*.

Others, like myself, are truly students. We teach from our process. Unlike the masters who embody the joy, bliss, and wisdom to which we all aspire, those of us who are students can spend much more time in the "unwanted" than we might like to admit. And yet, for me, the gift is that each of my challenges has led me to look deeper within. I don't usually write about these challenges because of my understanding of Law of Attraction. I acknowledge them briefly here because I want to personally encourage you. If you are facing your unique brand of difficulty, I want to suggest the possibility that right beside your suffering you may find your most profound enrichment.

By applying the principles I teach in this book, my life has turned itself inside out. I can find mystical realization at the center of a migraine. I can find peace at the center of a sleepless night. In fact, it is at the very extremes of the challenges that I live where I discover some of the most useful tools for daily life. These tools then carry me forward during more harmonious times. If you find usefulness here, I invite you to employ this system to help you navigate through your own challenges and to bring yourself to greater mastery in your own life. And there, you find joy regardless of circumstances.

You give me a gift by sharing in the gems that I have mined from the depths of my process. Thank you.

With Love and Appreciation,
Rebbie

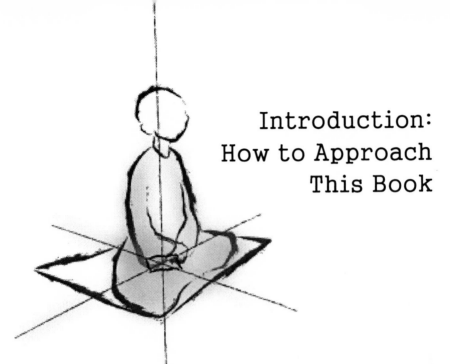

Introduction:
How to Approach
This Book

On an infinite path, one is always a beginner. So, I write this book from one beginner to another. As you walk through the circumstances of your life, I invite you to include this practice of inner alignment. It can bring joy, harmony, and success in any (and every) area of your life as a result. Miracles reveal themselves when you align your vision with your inner truth. This system empowers you to do just that. It guides you through a simple and express route to energetic alignment. Once you cultivate this inner alignment, you become a magnet for all the good you desire.

You Are the Garden

With the sun on your face, your hands in the earth, and your desire strong, you can grow just about anything, if you have the right seeds. The sweet fruits of the inner garden grow as naturally and as beautifully as their outer counterparts. The seeds of joy, love, and wisdom live inside of you. And while they will grow and flourish all on their own, with a little conscious cultivation these treasures of the inner garden blossom into respect and compassion, strong and satisfying relationships, success and prosperity, and a deep sense of global community.

You are the garden. Look around you. If you feel exhilarated, awed by the beauty, moved to tears of joy by the presence of life force within and around you, then the garden of your life serves you well. Peruse your life. Gaze at your environment, your relationships, and your posture. Notice your most prominent and frequent feeling tone. If you feel less than satisfied much of the time, consider looking inward. By taking some time to turn your attention away from outer circumstances, you can begin to align your personal consciousness and start reaping a more joyful, harmonious, love-filled life experience.

Three Ways to Use this Book

This book offers a system that can be used for three different purposes:

- For Spiritual Awareness
- For Healing
- For Joyful Manifestation

Spiritual Awareness

First, you can use this book to deepen your spiritual awareness. Whether or not you follow a specific spiritual path makes no difference. If you are deeply religious or if you reject religion completely, it really doesn't matter because the core of what we call spiritual is at the center of simply being human. This system can help you tap into the joy encoded in every moment. It helps you bring your individual consciousness into harmony with the transcendent Self.

It distills many of the ancient teachings of yoga down to their bare essence and offers practical uses for their wisdom.

If you are seeking to center yourself in an awareness of Spirit, God, Inner Being, Universal Intelligence, Infinite Consciousness, whatever you like to call the unnamable All, then you will find in this approach a way of thinking and a system of inner alignment that can guide you smoothly and successfully in that direction.

Healing

Another path you can take with this system leads to healing. If you suffer in your body, you no doubt feel an intense desire for healing. The physical and emotional pain brought on by illness can challenge even the hardiest of souls. This system provides tools that empower you to advance your own healing process from within.

While medical and natural healing practitioners can provide you with influential treatments, not one of them can do for you what you can do for yourself. No one else can choose your thoughts, your focus, or your interpretation of your emotions. The Yoga of Alignment embraces the perspective offered by Abraham[1], whose message we will look to often.

Law of Attraction

In order to navigate successfully through life's ups and downs to the place where your heart is always leading you, there is one simple piece of information that makes all the difference. With this effortless but life-altering shift in perspective, you can move forward with ease, clarity, and confidence toward the desires of your heart. In other words, you can get where you want to go on any subject. The information I'm talking about is Law of Attraction.

Abraham tells us that there is one universal law that is at the basis of all things. Law of Attraction, as it is called, causes things of a like vibration to be drawn together. Simply put, *like attracts like*.

Your life opens in ways you may not previously have been able to imagine when you integrate into your awareness these three attributes of Law of Attraction:

- It is eternally consistent.
- It applies to all things physical and nonphysical.
- It sits silently at the center of your world holding everything together.

Law of Attraction is to you what gravity is to the earth. It brings things to you. It carries into your life and into your awareness all things that match your vibration. The more deeply you can integrate this principle into your conscious awareness, the greater creative freedom you can find in your experience of living life as a human being. The more free you feel, the more generous you become. The more generous you become, the happier you feel.

The ultimate generosity is the generosity of the heart. It is the free offering of love. And love is a mystical entity that follows a paradoxical law of economy. The more you give it away, the more you have.

Living in harmony with Law of Attraction leads to a life of abundance. Very specific abundance. Abundance of things, people, and experiences that you love. It leads to a life filled with all that your heart desires. *Your* heart. Not someone else's heart. Not what someone else told you your heart *should* desire. Living in harmony with Law of Attraction leads to a life filled with satisfying moments for your soul.

You trust gravity implicitly. You don't even have to think about it. You include it masterfully in all your unconscious calculations as you move through the physical universe. It is our intention in the Yoga of Alignment to come to trust Law of Attraction with the same conviction and the same natural ease with which we trust gravity.

Once you recognize the intimate relationship you have with Law of Attraction, you will see why we do this work. It is the most obvious and natural corollary that if we participate with this attractive force it responds consistently. Of course you could deny it, but that would be like denying gravity. You'd end up sweeping up a lot of broken glass at the end of each day, and you'd wonder why all your nice fancy things keep smashing to the ground. Once you would include gravity in your plans, your life experience would be a smoother and more satisfying journey.

Abraham's contribution to the Yoga of Alignment (YOFA™) training cannot be overstated. It is at the heart of everything we are doing in this system. My appreciation for Jerry and Esther Hicks overflows and the love I feel for Abraham and the value I perceive in their magnificent message flows on and on. It grows stronger and stronger and runs deeper and deeper all the time. I encourage you to learn from them directly through their writings and recordings as you move through this system. Their contact information is listed in the notes at the end of this chapter.

Whether you are focused upon your spiritual journey, your healing, or your experiences in the world, Law of Attraction is always responding to your vibration and matching it. How you focus your attention creates a point of attraction and that in turn determines the experience you are living. Abraham tells us that no one can choose your vibrational point of attraction but you. If you try to shift your point of attraction all at once, when you've got Law of Attraction working on all your old habitual thoughts, you may begin to feel frustrated or overwhelmed. That's why we do this as a soft and gradual process. Always feeling our way through, knowing that inner guidance is our constant companion, we find our way. While experimenting with different perspectives, the true indication that you have found a better alternative in your thinking is that it feels a little bit better when you consider it.

When healing is our desire, navigating through the current patterns set in motion by old repeated thought forms requires a completely different focus. It requires an unwavering commitment to thoughts that bring joy. That is not an easy task during a period of illness. Therefore, in difficult times, we can translate "thoughts that bring joy" to "thoughts that bring relief."

In either case, this boils down to releasing resistant thoughts. Thoughts that bring relief provide a little opening for life force to flow through. If you were already feeling pretty good to begin with, that opening feels like joy. If you were suffering, it feels like relief. Either way, it is welcome.

This system provides a way for you to carry yourself smoothly and safely through the patterns of your own thoughts without getting entangled in their content. As with any system of healing, stepping into health will be instantaneous for some, more drawn out for others. In either case, setting this process in motion brings you closer to the freedom and health that you seek.

What about when pain is not physical? Depression, anxiety, anger, and addiction indicate counter-currents that interfere with your natural sense of well-being. If you are troubled by undesirable emotions or plagued by your own unintentional behaviors, there is some good news for you.

I like the metaphor used by Abraham, who talks about "floating your cork." If you hold a cork under water, it stays submerged only as long as you hold it down. But as soon as you release it, the cork floats back up. Emotional buoyancy acts in exactly the same way. When you learn these methods of allowing the flow of life force to move through you, you bob right back up to the surface effortlessly. You will feel great relief when you directly experience the joy, love, and peace that are your natural state.

You don't need to invent or create your happiness. It is always there. When you access it, life feels wonderful. That feeling makes you want to live forever. While this system does not promise a cure for your addictions or an immediate lifting of your depression, it does hold one guarantee. To the degree that you bring yourself into alignment, you will notice small improvements. With consistent practice, these small moments of relief will last longer and become more frequent. As you realize that you have the power to make changes that improve your emotional state, you will make them faster and with more precision.

If physical or emotional healing is what you are looking for, this approach offers assistance in a way that may be new to you. Instead of listing cookbook style remedies for conditions and syndromes, this system is purely wholistic. That means you will be guided toward developing trust in your own natural healing ability. You will start to make friends with your own Innate Intelligence. In fact, you will put it in charge of your healing no matter how superficial or severe your condition may seem, and no matter how many other treatments you may have going on at the same time. In this system, we neither diagnose nor treat. What we do is clear the channels where the flow of life force has been obstructed. By allowing the flow of life force to enter where it had been blocked, we support your healing.

Joyful Manifestation

The third direction you can take with this system guides you to the fruition of your dreams. Career, relationships, possessions, and all the things and activities that make up a life are fair game in this portion of the system. Here you can bring your hopes and dreams into the sunlight and see which ones really ring your bells. Then you can use the principles of the Yoga of Alignment to begin setting into motion the creation of that which you truly desire.

Maybe you have some old programming that says it is materialistic and selfish to try to create wealth or an abundance of material things. But once you realize that you are always involved in creating your reality, wanted or unwanted, it begins to make sense to direct your creative energies in a direction that pleases you rather than in one that brings you into more struggle.

Although possessions will not bring you lasting happiness, the creative process draws life force through you in ways that enliven and energize you. With this system, you find yourself beginning to naturally flow your life in the direction of success and prosperity, if for no other reason than for the joy of the journey. If you are looking for a relationship, or to harmonize the one you've got, this is also the aspect of this system that gets you where you want to go.

Once you begin clearing the way and allowing life force to flow freely in these three directions (spirituality, healing, and joyful manifestation), you can choose which one you want to work with at any time. You can use the exercises in this book to establish your spiritual connection first thing in the morning, focus on your career during the day, and initiate healing before going to bed. The tools are in your hands and you can customize the system to suit your needs. Just as in the garden, where you spend some of your time planting seeds and some of your time pulling weeds, in your inner garden you will follow the needs of the moment and use whatever part of the system serves you best in your *now*.

The Mystical Experience

We want to experience life fully, freely, purely, and joyfully, but often we miss the mark. What gets in the way? Very often it is our own outwardly focused thinking that leads us to conclusions that do not serve us. We think we see the whole picture but we are missing large pieces of the puzzle. Then we speak or behave in ways that take us in the opposite direction of where we want to go. Although we have access to all knowing, we tend to live our lives repeatedly using the same few habitual beliefs to get us through all situations. Opening to inner knowing can make all the difference between a frustrating life experience and one that flows. Sometimes the answer is right inside of us but we cannot see it because of our habitual patterns of belief.

As a child you probably had a sense of awe, a deep, unworded understanding of the connectedness of all things. You may even have tried to communicate your mystical revelations to some grown-ups. I was blessed with older sisters who appreciated and encouraged my perceptions. Probably many of you, like me, have traveled a somewhat mystical path from an early age. If you did not have the good fortune of having like-minded adults in your circle, your most sacred inner moments might have been dismissed, even ridiculed. You probably don't remember the point at which you closed down your mystical nature. In the YOFA™ system, you will have the opportunity to reconnect with, or expand, your own unique inner knowing.

The goal of this book is to offer you a process for aligning your energy in such a way that you can easily access your own direct experience (rather than learned knowledge) of universal realities. Mystical truths have always revealed themselves directly to those who could recognize them. Those with the ability to receive this extraordinary information and communicate it have then taught the rest of us. As you work with this system and the mystical experience becomes a more regular part of your day, you can find more of your own answers, participate more in your own healing, and enjoy more of the blessings that come from finding energetic alignment with your inner Self.

You don't need to be a genius or a spiritual guru to share in these simple yet seemingly magical revelations about life. As human beings, we all share certain qualities that unite us. Understanding some of our common energy patterns allows us to know ourselves better, to create healing from within, and to link ourselves to each other in a way that transcends race, color, religion, or even generations of enmity. This system fosters respect for the divinity within all of us and compassion for our humanity, with all its challenges.

Is This Book for You?

Whether you come to this book with years of experience in meditation or none at all, this system can serve you. All you really need is a desire and a willingness to begin this process precisely where you now stand. From there, you can step purely into your practice of inner alignment. Since everyone's inner life is unique, your experiences with this work will be yours and yours alone. There is no right or wrong. Only you know the healing you desire. Only you know the desire that moves you to quiet the mind and seek whatever it is that you seek. The journey is a very personal one.

If this is your first glance inward, if you have never tried any form of meditation before, welcome to the garden. With no preconceived ideas, no over-intellectualizations, you are in the perfect place to follow these instructions and fill your baskets high at harvest time. This book will take you through the basics of inner alignment and it will introduce you to a system that you can use for years to come. It will also prepare you well should you decide to move on to (or return to) any other type of meditation. You can think of this process as preparation for meditation. In the end, it becomes meditation in itself. Your completion of this course will give you basic training in accessing your mystical nature. This is not an exploration of the occult or supernatural. Rather, this system teaches you to intuitively reconnect with your inner being. From there you can tap into the natural knowing, being, and full, joyful living that have always been yours.

If you are a long-time meditator, a scholar of Eastern mysticism, or a trained practitioner of the healing arts, you might be wondering what this book has to offer you. If you come to this system with much knowledge and experience, you can use this system for fine-tuning. The combination of teachings that join together to form this particular approach can help you deepen your authenticity and more purely follow the path you have already embraced.

This system is compatible with other forms of meditation and provides a friendly form of preparation for many other types of inner work. By aligning your consciousness and bringing yourself to a state of inner harmony before focusing on your breath, mantra, movement, etc., you will find more awareness, more flow, and less resistance in the process. The Yoga of Alignment exercises can function as an adapter between the active mental state of your day and the mind-quieting process of meditation. It can blend your states so that you move more smoothly to and from your regular form of meditation. Many people avoid meditating because shifting from the fast pace of daily activities to the stillness and quiet of the cushion is too abrupt and jarring. These exercises help you down-shift gently so you glide into heightened awareness in meditation, rather than crashing into your thoughts at high speed.

For those in the healing professions, this practice can serve you well. Preparing yourself energetically before seeing patients or clients allows you to see both the problem and the solution more clearly. It allows you to be more connected and authentic with your patients. Your mere presence becomes conducive to healing. Likewise, if you are a patient, aligning yourself before seeing your doctor may help you verbalize your condition in a way that can be better heard. It may help your healing practitioner see and offer more clearly that which you need to support your healing.

No matter what your previous experience has been, coming to this work with your current needs and desires in focus will no doubt reveal to you the most useful aspect of this material for you. If you choose to do this with a partner or in a group, you may be amazed at how different the focus turns out to be for each of you. Every garden has its own charm, its own beauty, and its own challenges. Whether you do this with others or alone, there are two agreements that will increase your results exponentially. The same plant that produced 10 tomatoes may produce 100 if properly fertilized. You can fertilize your inner garden with these two simple agreements.

Make These Two Agreements First

Before you lift your hoe or sprinkle your seeds, let me tell you how to guarantee results. If you do nothing but make these two agreements, you will benefit in countless ways. If you fertilize your garden with these two agreements, you will grow the most colorful flowers, harvest the most delicious fruits, and produce the most potent medicinal herbs.

These two agreements, simply stated are:

1. Honor the divinity in everyone including yourself.
2. Have compassion for the humanity in everyone including yourself.

By remembering and keeping these two agreements, you are developing a transformational habit. We all know the bumpy road of unwanted, automatic thinking and doing we call *habits*. Imagine how beneficial a life affirming habit can be. Imagine the kindness you can exchange with others, the love that can flow, and the fun and laughter that can erupt when you have a strong, automatic habit of thinking and doing that effortlessly moves you in the direction you want to go.

Honoring the divinity in everyone can really challenge your imagination. Go to a department store or ride on public transportation. Sit face to face with strangers and remind yourself of their divinity. Look at your neighbors, coworkers, religious leaders, teachers, politicians, and parents. Look at people of different races, different beliefs, and different lifestyles. Look at people who may not choose to honor you, even criminals. When you can honor the divinity in all of them, your garden bursts with color. Your life force increases. Don't forget to include yourself in the mix. All shimmering slivers of God-stuff surround you, each with a different face, a different voice, and a different perspective. Taking the time to honor the divinity in everyone you encounter can radically change your feeling about the world in which you live and make it a more majestic dwelling place.

As you go searching for the divine spark in your bus driver and your mother-in-law, you will surely also encounter their human aspect. We've all got a limited instrument through which to perceive and respond to the universe and each other. We frequently bump into others' limitations with our own.

Having compassion for the frailties and imperfections in the human aspect of everyone you meet can be equally challenging, especially when you feel hurt or attacked by someone. It helps to know that anyone who is in a pure state of alignment with their inner Self would not intentionally want to hurt you. In fact, the acts of aggression that are so hard to forgive are the evidence of the pain and energetic disharmony of the aggressor. Because of the limits of our perspective as human beings, we include an aspect that always stands incomplete, imperfect, and vulnerable. Understanding this gives us a constant opportunity to see others and ourselves through the forgiving eyes of compassion. Although not always easy, it is excellent fertilizer for our inner garden.

By accepting these two agreements, you embrace your dual nature. You are both divine and human, perfect and imperfect, infinite and finite, joyful and suffering. By remembering to extend these agreements to yourself, you open the doors for healing. Train yourself to honor your own divinity and have compassion for your own humanity. Study this in yourself. Memorize it. Use it. Friends will admire the flowers in your garden. You will smell fragrant. You will glow with equanimity.

Getting Your Hands Dirty

Dig in. No gloves. Feel the ground of your being. Since you are the garden, this book is all about you. In the first section you learn the basic premise of this system including the concepts of flow and alignment. You learn how to sit and how to apply the core components of inner alignment. When you get to the second section, be ready to begin tending the garden. With the help of the exercises, sitting upright and still, you touch the miracle of life with your attention. From deep within the mystery of your consciousness, a relationship between your individual identity and your transcendent Self takes the foreground. You gain a thorough knowledge, both conceptually and experientially, of the nature of your uniquely human root. By the time you reach the third section, you will have gained momentum and experience with this work. The principles of creativity, desire, power, ego, love, communication, and wisdom that arise in the remaining chakras take on new meaning. In the fourth section, you begin to turn your new discoveries into practical techniques for enriching your life.

Once you finish the book, your process re-begins. I encourage you to experiment. Make it your own. Use the tools offered in this book to design the garden that reflects your true, authentic self, the garden that is you.

Chapter Notes

---

[1] You can find out all about the teachings of Abraham at the official Abraham-Hicks website at www.abraham-hicks.com or contact Abraham-Hicks Publications, P.O. Box 690070 , San Antonio, TX 78269, Phone: 830-755-2299, Fax: 830-755-4179

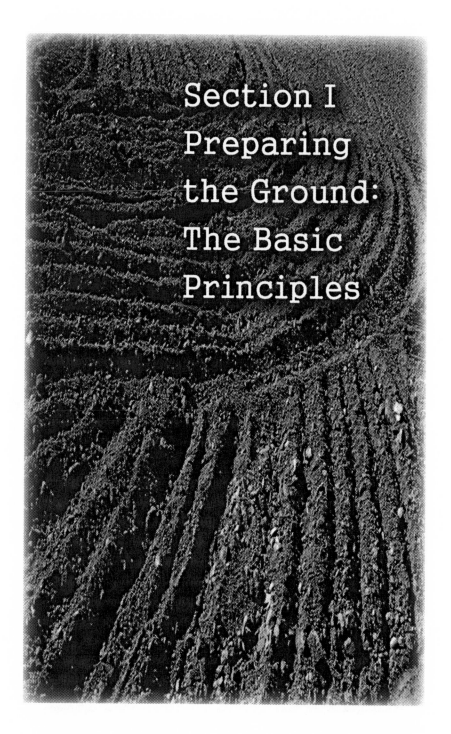

Section I
Preparing
the Ground:
The Basic
Principles

Chapter 1
Let the
Water Flow:
Life Force

You probably picked up this book because you want to make your life better. You are seeking something intangible and your inner wisdom has sent you out to find some direction, some friendly advice, a trustworthy travel companion. As we travel together through this system that I am calling the Yoga of Alignment (YOFA™), I hope to be just that to you: a friend when you are in need, a guide when you are lost, a fellow traveler who also benefits from your company.

I, like you, have worked in many different ways to improve my life. Whether it meant pursuing higher education or working harder at my job, whether it involved practicing prayer or meditation, I have found one thing to be true. To the degree that I carried out these "virtuous" activities with internal conflict, they brought more dissatisfaction. To the degree that I was in harmony with myself as I did them, all of these efforts were supremely rewarding.

How can we intentionally align ourselves so that we no longer have to rely on what we think of as chance or luck for our good fortune? This book offers one such method. With the Yoga of Alignment, you will learn to align your awareness so that your many efforts in life may meet with greater success.

If you approach this system hoping that it will bring lasting happiness, I ask you to pause and consider the following: The happiness that you seek already exists inside of you. You may search for it in new possessions, in a new romance, or even in a new book. But the most these externals can do is to reflect back to you the brilliant happiness that is innately yours.

An ancient Indian fable tells the story of a musk deer that emits the fragrance of musk from a spot on his forehead. The deer runs around frantically looking for the delightful scent, never realizing it is his own fragrance that he seeks. He will even jump off a cliff chasing after that which already resides within him. In the same way, you and I run after happiness thinking we will find it outside ourselves. We may even have a conscious philosophy that tells us otherwise, but still, how do we find the happiness within? That is the subject of this book. We begin with one simple idea:

You are the garden.

The outer garden is most famous for its beauty. The inner garden is invisible. Why grow flowers that no one can see? Why harvest fruits that cannot be eaten? For one simple reason. Tending the garden within gives us access to the happiness we seek. Since gardening is a cyclic process, we can jump in wherever we are. Let's begin right now with this simple fact:

The garden needs water.

Nothing else will do. Pure, sparkling, clear-flowing water provides our image for the invisible, ever-flowing presence of life force. In order to have a lush and colorful life experience, in order to cultivate a deeply satisfying sense of Inner Being or Self, we must allow its flow within us as life force.

Life force manifests as joy. Joy flourishes into vibrant health. Joy brings unconditional love to all relationships. Joy loves work and loves play. Joy attracts an abundance of things wanted. Joy flows like water and nourishes our inner garden. As long as the garden gets a good downpour every now and then, there is really nothing else we need to do about it. With life force flowing from above like rain, we can relax and let the garden grow.

Yet we all have dry spells. These are times when we knowingly or unknowingly block ourselves off from the flood of life force that would otherwise nurture our lives. In the physical garden, the plants wilt without water. In our lives, we see disharmony in our relationships, failed health, or a feeling of emptiness, depression, or anxiety when we are cut off from the flow of life force. With this system, you begin to allow that flow where it previously had been blocked. The garden of your life can then flourish.

What is life force, anyway? It goes by many names but they all boil down to the same thing. Its source is Universal Intelligence. At least that's what chiropractors tend to call it. In your place of worship you may call it God. Philosophers may call it Nature. It can be thought of as the power that generates all the known and unknown forces and laws of the universe. It is the supreme consciousness, the one mind, the singular unifying intelligence, the incomprehensible organizing force that holds the stars in place, keeps the electrons spinning in their orbits, and sources everything in between and beyond. It includes the laws of physics as well as the laws of spirit.

It is beyond our capacity to understand, fully experience, or express. Swami Sivananda has said, "To define God is to deny God." With this understanding, we proceed, using words as best we can to further us along our way.

This incomprehensible Universal Intelligence, call it what you will, sources what we are calling life force. It is creative and it plays no favorites. It devotes as much care and detail to the creation of a galaxy as it does to an atom. It continually births the universe as we know it and beyond. When this awe-inspiring presence focuses itself as life, you and I come into the picture. We are the miracle of life, though we rarely recognize the personal attention that went into our creation and that continually maintains us. This branch of Universal Intelligence that is devoted to birthing, organizing, and sustaining life, we call *Innate Intelligence* or *life force*.

Innate Intelligence expresses as cells and organs. It grows hair and it bursts out as laughter. It can read while digesting. It can play tennis while repairing cells. This is the amazing power within us. Life force will bring our inner garden to its greatest fulfillment. Life force made us. It heals us. It always knows just what to do. Forever continuous with its universal source, it always acts appropriately. *It always does good for the life it flows through.*

We want this force pouring into our garden. This water lifts us to the heights of living that we seek. Without it we suffer, and yet ironically, it is always available. We just need to let it flow. Let's look at three different versions of this story. I'm sure you can come up with many more. Each of these tells us the water is already there, just waiting for us to allow it in. The first model helps us heal. The second cultivates spiritual awareness. The third leads to joyful success in our human endeavors.

Healing

In my first semester of chiropractic school in 1980, I sat with about 120 others in a large classroom and listened to the principles of chiropractic philosophy. One of the simplest and most important concepts they taught us then provides us now with the basis for the healing branch of this system:

Healing always comes from within.

If you are looking to this system for healing, a good place to begin is right here with this notion:

- No medicine, treatment, or "healer" heals you.

- Healing always and exclusively comes from within you, orchestrated by your own flow of life force.

That's why we want to make sure that this energy flows abundantly in your life. It can work with other treatments, but without it, no other treatment can work. If you have been a chiropractic patient or if you are a chiropractor or practitioner of another healing art that holds a similar philosophy, then none of this is new to you. If, on the other hand, this is the first time you have encountered this point of view, you still may not be convinced of the crucial role in healing played by the flow of life force. You can prove this principle to yourself with the following experiment.

Take a raw piece of meat. Cut it with a knife. Put any kind of ointment you like on it, bandage it, and leave it for a few days. See if it heals. It will not. You and I have had numerous cuts and worse that have healed and are long forgotten, but the meat will not heal. The difference is simple. No life force, no healing. This mysterious component that is present in all life still eludes us. We still stumble over the concept. It's not scientific enough for us. But the fact is, life force is undeniable. When it pours into our garden we thrive.

Years ago, many "old time" chiropractors explained chiropractic to their patients by comparing the nerves of the body to a garden hose. They compared the life force flowing through the nerves to the water flowing through the hose. They said that if you step on the hose, you stop the flow of water in the same way that a misaligned spinal bone pressing on a nerve stops the flow of life force to the rest of the body.

This analogy fell fiercely out of fashion because, from a physiological standpoint, it was inaccurate.[1] While it is true that this explanation didn't teach anyone the physiology of nerve cells or the complexities of the inflammatory process, it did do something else. It taught people the importance of flow. While it may not have been physiologically accurate, it was descriptive of an energetic reality. Since we are focused on energy here, let's consider it.

These early pioneers spoke very clearly in the language of images. With their simple reference to a common garden hose, they made crystal clear what a long dissertation on inflamed neural sheaths and altered release of neurotransmitters would struggle to communicate. When you hold a garden hose on a hot summer day and watch the water pouring onto the dry cracked soil around your plant, you can feel the meaning of the word flow. When you find yourself weak and drained and then a chiropractic adjustment or some other process of alignment restores your energy, you can feel the flow of life force restored within you.

Chiropractic began with the simple original intention to restore the flow of life force for the purpose of healing. But as it has achieved greater acceptance in the mainstream, the philosophy of flow has sometimes gotten lost in the shuffle. Now, as you and I practice the Yoga of Alignment together, we will place chiropractic philosophy in the spotlight and distill it down to its energetic principles. We will focus on these principles as we apply them to the energetic counterpart of the physical spine, which we will call the *energetic spine*.

Because of my long association with chiropractic as a wholistic healing art, I sometimes forget that many people think of chiropractic as a mere treatment for back pain. If you find yourself in this category, you may be surprised to find out that the first chiropractic adjustment in 1895 did not aim to relieve anyone's back pain. Instead it restored the hearing of a man who had been deaf for 17 years. As hard as it may be to imagine, in its inception, chiropractic became known as a treatment for deafness. Once the mechanism of the chiropractic adjustment was better understood, this new healing art began helping people with just about every type of health problem.

If you are unfamiliar with the energy-based principles of chiropractic, then you are probably not used to thinking about the spine in such a globally important way. Fortunately, you don't have to study all the anatomy and physiology of the physical spine in order to learn this system and enjoy the benefits of life force flowing through your energetic spine. We can just dip lightly into the principles of chiropractic to help guide us. Very simply, the philosophy of chiropractic, which flows through the center of the Yoga of Alignment, can be summed up in 4 statements:

1. Life force flows from its universal source through the spine to all parts of your body.[2]
2. Life force orchestrates all functioning and healing.
3. If the flow of life force becomes interrupted, the body will have difficulty functioning and/or healing.
4. Aligning the spine restores the flow of life force so the body can heal itself.

That's pretty simple. Chiropractic, based on the alignment of the spine, has restored eyesight, hearing, and general health to people suffering from almost every illness imaginable. It has done this time after time, by removing the obstacles and allowing the person's own healing power (life force) to flow and heal them. Why don't we put these simple principles to use for ourselves in our quest to attain and maintain vibrant health? Align the spine, remove obstructions to the flow of life force, and let the body heal itself. The healing power housed in the spine must not be underestimated. It provides the main avenue of flow for the healing power resident in the living being, which is beyond measure.

With all this in mind, we can describe what we are doing in this branch of the Yoga of Alignment as taking our foot off the hose. We are learning techniques designed to align the energetic spine so that life force can flow freely and the body can heal itself. Of the three branches of this system, here we learn to let the water flow for the purpose of healing.

Spiritual Awareness

Long before I sat in a chiropractic classroom, I sat on the floor of Saint Luke's Church in Manhattan's West Village. It was the early 1970's and hundreds of seekers, young and old, sat transfixed every Thursday night as Hilda[3], known as a healer and "holy lady" in those days, taught us the essence of yoga. I was only 17 or so, but I listened carefully and meditated intensely. What I learned from Hilda's meetings profoundly influenced the course of my life.

Thursday nights became a highlight of my week in a time darkened by tragedy in my family. The path of Bhakti, the yoga of love and devotion, offered me great comfort in the face of profound sadness and I established a relationship with the divine in those years that has never left me.

But the intensity of my youthful, spiritual fervor often got me in trouble. More than once Hilda came to my home to help me through some spiritual crisis. I can still hear the traces of her English accent, "Don't meditate, dear! Go out and play with the other kids!" She called everybody "kids."

I didn't listen to her. I kept meditating. But the path was not easy for me and over the decades between then and now, I have had a stormy relationship with the process of meditation. Unlike many who found peace and contentment on their meditation cushion, I struggled for many years. At different times in my life I took Hilda's advice and stopped trying altogether. The system offered in this book has brought me into greater harmony with myself and with my Self. Now, the value of sitting in meditation has become clear and palpable in my life. And although I can still completely succumb to distraction, I have learned to be more gentle with myself. And while I still can blow my own circuits at times, accessing more energy than my system can handle, I am beginning to learn the paradoxical lesson. When that happens I simply stop and go play with the other "kids."

One of Hilda's lessons felt extremely important to me back then and it provides the spiritual basis of this system for us now:

Let the water flow and God will make the flowers grow.

In this lesson, Hilda clearly described the spiritual aspect of our inner garden. She told us to take a hoe and push the dirt away. I had never tended a real garden back then. I lived on the Upper West Side of Manhattan. The closest experience I had to that of tending a garden was the appreciation I felt for the trees on the sidewalk, growing through open squares in the cement. But I understood when she told us to make a channel for the water to flow directly to the garden. She made it clear that our job is not to make the flowers grow. We need only allow the water, the life force, Innate Intelligence to flow. "Let the water flow and God will make the flowers grow." That was the lesson.

Just as the chiropractic model of the flow of water (life force) gave us the formula for healing in the inner garden, yoga provides us with the spiritual model of flow. Both chiropractic and yoga speak of the same water, the same life force, the same flow, but here we seek that flow for the purpose of spiritual connection with Source.

When I sat in Hilda's presence, her lesson was immediate and practical. Years later I found this same lesson in a verse of Patanjali's Yoga Sutras. Sri Swami Satchidananda spells it out clearly in his commentary on the Yoga Sutras[4]:

> "Here Patanjali gives a nice example of how a farmer allows the water to run into his field simply by removing the obstacles in his water course. Your mind also wants to run to its original source of tranquility, but there are impediments on the way which obstruct the flow... Water is always running in the canal. The cultivator simply goes looking for some obstacles and takes them out. Once he removes them he doesn't

need to tell the water it can flow. It is like the sun outside; it is always there, ready to come into your house. The obstacles are the closed doors and windows. If you simply open them, the light shines in."

We have already described our activity in the Yoga of Alignment as taking our foot off the hose. A second way to describe our efforts here would be to say we are removing obstacles so that the water can flow in our spiritual lives. In this branch of the system, we will be learning to align the energetic spine in order to let the water flow for the purpose of union with God (or whatever name or silence you may use for that supreme presence.) We will look to many schools of yoga for guidance in this pursuit.

The Meaning of Success is Joy

In 1993 a dear friend convinced me to go to an Abraham[5] workshop. I still have not stopped thanking her for finding a way to get through to me on this subject. Abraham largely teaches in a question and answer format. On several occasions, back when I was first listening, I heard participants tell Abraham that they were not open to the idea of channeling. Abraham typically answered, "We aren't either." The room filled with laughter that diffused the resistant state anyone may have held around this strange subject. With that out of the way, the message could be heard more clearly. The teachings of Abraham, as offered by Jerry and Esther Hicks, form the third leg of the tripod of the Yoga of Alignment.

When I first came to this material, Abraham was talking much about the importance of having an *open valve*. They were saying that pure positive energy (another name for life force), like water, presses against your valve. All you need to do is open your valve to have this life force flow through you. As you can imagine, when you close your valve (as we so often do) you block off the flow of life force and "pinch yourself off from the stream of well-being," as Abraham has described it. Of course, you never fully close your valve, but if the trickle gets too thin, it can translate into ill health, failed relationships, or any other form of getting what you don't want or not getting what you do want. Abraham encourages us to keep our valve open, regardless of circumstances. This way, we become joyful, strong, and healthy. With our valve open and our joy accessible, we can more consistently manifest that which we desire as our life unfolds. Through the teachings of Abraham, we learn to let the water flow once again. This time the purpose is a joyful unfolding of life.

Just as the outer garden needs water, the inner garden relies on the flow of life force. Chiropractic teaches us the importance of this flow for healing. Yoga teaches us the same priority for spiritual awareness. Abraham reiterates this lesson for achieving success and joy in life. These three voices join together here to amplify the message: The cause of most spiritual, physical, and emotional problems can be traced to an obstruction in the flow of life force. The solution in each case is the same:

Let the water flow.

Chapter Notes

[1] For current chiropractic research, refer to the work of Bruce Lipton, Ph.D. http://www.brucelipton.com and David Seaman, D.C.

[2] Life force flows directly to every cell of your body. This system focuses on the particular pathway that flows through the energetic counterpart of the spine.

[3] Hilda Charlton taught spiritual classes in New York City for 23 years. Her numerous books and tapes are available from Golden Quest Publications at www.hildacharlton.com.

[4] From Integral Yoga, The Yoga Sutras of Patanjali, Translation and Commentary by Sri Swami Satchidananda. Integral Yoga Publications, Yogaville, Virginia, 1978. Book 4, Verse 3, page 239.

[5] Abraham is described on the official Abraham-Hicks website as follows: "Abraham, a group of obviously evolved teachers, speak their broader Non-physical perspective through the physical apparatus of Esther. Speaking to our level of comprehension, from their present moment to our now, through a series of loving, allowing, brilliant yet comprehensively simple, recordings in print and in sound -- they guide us to a clear connection with our Inner Being -- they guide us to self-upliftment from our total self." To find the schedule of upcoming Abraham Workshops, visit www.abraham-hicks.com.

Chapter 2
Clearing
the Path:
Alignment

We have already identified our one main objective in this system: Letting the water flow in the garden. That means allowing life force to flow through every aspect of our lives. In order for the water to flow, it must have a clear path through which to flow. If chaotic and conflicting forces impede its flow, the garden will dry up. You can tell this is happening when your relationships become strained, depression or anxiety rules your emotions, or any other symptom of dis-ease keeps grabbing your attention. We can dissolve these patterns of resistance and ensure a generous flow of life force by achieving inner alignment.

You may have come to this system in search of heightened spiritual awareness or looking for the answer to a specific personal problem. Regardless of what brought you here, your ability to align your energy for the purpose of allowing life force to flow through you will be the measure of your success with this approach. Alignment is our method and we will be looking at it from many different angles. Not only will we be working with it in the realm of ideas and concepts, but we will also approach it experientially. Ultimately, we reap many benefits from this effort.

What is Alignment?

Since I am a chiropractor, the word alignment conjures up vertebrae, discs, and adjustments in my mind. If you work in graphics, maybe your mind flashes to margins, crop marks, and rulers. My farmer friend marks rows in the field with an old red tractor and creates alignment in the random countryside. These physical examples of alignment do their job by bringing their varied subjects into a straight line.

Physical alignment fosters a certain type of flow. We are familiar with different types of flow like the movement of traffic on our roads, the flow of merchandise in our stores, and the flow of water through the garden hose. In this system, we look past the physical into the energetic aspects of alignment and flow. Energetic alignment brings another dimension of beneficial attributes to our lives. We can start with these four notions: wholeness, purity, magnetism, and union. Let's take these one at a time.

> *Wholeness* – By aligning yourself from within, you move toward experiencing your wholeness. No longer split into competing factions, your entire being functions with a unified intention. This way of living promotes health, happiness, simplicity, and power.

> *Purity* – By freeing yourself from conflicting emotions and contradictory intentions, your voice becomes pure, your message becomes clear, and all stress leaves your system. You become lighter, swifter, calmer, and more confident.

> *Magnetism* – The alignment of the electrons in the atoms of a magnet generates an attractive force around that magnet. Aligning with your true nature attracts to you all that is harmonious with your essential Self. You be-

come a powerful magnet drawing to you that which your heart truly desires.

Union – Aligning your individual sense of self with your Higher Self or God makes you more like that which you seek, and ultimately leads to union. No longer a disconnected and struggling lost soul, you find your opening to Source, and all that you need flows to you and through you with ease.

Abraham has said, "If you will let the thing that is most important to you be your alignment to who you are, your alignment to Source, then every desire that is born out of this magnificent contrasting experience will flow easily to you."[1]

Let's explore a few forms of alignment. Ultimately, we will set our gaze far beyond the physical alignment of the spine, but the physical spine remains an excellent place to begin our journey.

What's in a Spine?

We don't usually pay much attention to the spine unless it is causing us pain. Backaches, sciatica, and whiplash get our attention, but the quiet miracle of the "well-oiled" spine typically goes unnoticed.

As we move further into the energetic wonders of the spine and its relationship to consciousness, it becomes advantageous for us to know certain basics about the physical spine. A little grounding in anatomy will anchor us in the body so that we can sail farther in consciousness without getting lost.

The spinal column is typically divided into five sections. From bottom to top they are:

- The coccyx or tail bone
- The sacrum located in the pelvis

- The lumbar spine or lower back
- The thoracic spine or mid back
- The cervical spine or neck

The coccyx and sacrum begin as several separate bones, but by adulthood each fuses into a singular bone. The lumbar spine remains 5 bones, the thoracic 12, and the cervical 7. I want to tell you something about these 26 bones. No two are alike. Each has its own personality, its own geometry, and its own function. We won't examine each bone here, but if you swing your hand around behind your back and run your fingers across the bones of your spine, you can begin to get a sense of a world of activity, precision, and power right inside of you.

Let's return to the idea of a magnet for a minute. The magnet gets its power from the alignment of its electrons. One way to demagnetize a magnet, or to greatly reduce its power, is to drop it. When you drop a magnet you scramble the arrangement of its electrons. Your once powerful magnet now becomes an ordinary piece of metal.

Our beautifully arranged spine shifts in and out of alignment with every bump and tumble we endure. Even the repetitive micro-traumas of carrying a backpack or briefcase, or of such common stressors as driving or typing, activities that seem innocent enough, can put a strain on our alignment. These daily stresses, or the amplification of gravity's influence on our structure, can have the effect of "demagnetizing" us.

Obviously, we are not bar magnets and the misalignment of our spine will not suddenly drop paperclips from our effortless grip, but much of the functioning of our nervous system depends on the proper alignment of the spine. The spinal nerves that carry information to and from the rest of the body must make their way in and out of the portals of the spine without interference. If the spine loses its proper alignment, irritation to the nearby nerves can cause a distortion of signals.

When we begin the meditative practice of alignment, physical alignment plays an important role. The position of the spinal bones, sitting one on top of the other, sets the stage for the higher octaves of alignment we seek. In our exploration of energy centers, we investigate different levels of alignment for the sake of spiritual upliftment, deep healing, and experiencing greater joy in the world. This adventure into the energetic realm of consciousness does not replace its physical counterpart. If you practice Hatha Yoga, regularly visit the chiropractor, or engage in any other activities that promote spinal alignment, you will augment the benefits of the work you do here. All practices of alignment are mutually beneficial.

Spine Waves

Did your mother ever tell you to "stand up straight"? Mine sure did. But where there's a will to slump, there's usually a way. I managed to droop my adolescent shoulders even within the confines of an orthopedic strap that aimed to pull my shoulders back and keep me itchy all day long. Fortunately, my parents saw the futility of this contraption and released me from its grip pretty quickly. I now understand that a system of energetic alignment would have been more effective for me back then. Although my posture is far from exemplary, the Yoga of Alignment meditations have lifted my spine more than any other method I have ever explored.

What my mother realized intuitively was that the imbalance in my posture was blocking my energy flow. In her motherly love, she wanted to help me. But in the time-honored ritual between adolescent and parent, we missed each other's messages and I slumped my way through much of life.

Contraptions and parental reminders may work in some cases, and if they do, the energy flow will probably follow, but the system you will be learning in this book works in the opposite direction.

It works from the inside out. We will get the energy flowing and behold an effortless change in posture.

In either case, when you "stand up straight," although your posture may look strictly upright, your spine itself must maintain its curves in order to function optimally. Although anatomists and chiropractors usually talk about the three curves of the spine, we include the head and the pelvis and talk about five curves. Rather than thinking of the bones of the spine as static pieces of matter shaped in curves, we think of the spine as a wave.

A wave moves. It transfers energy from one place to another. Our beloved wave guru, the ocean, moves continuously. It is anything but static. In order to help us leave behind our old, hardened ideas about the spine and open to a sense of the spine as a wave, let's shift the spine into alignment with the ocean waves by bringing it to the horizontal plane.

If you imagine lying on your back and asking a friend to look at you with x-ray vision, your friend will see the wavy up-down pattern of the well known spinal curves within you. She will see the high points and low points of your spine wave. I'm giving her the liberty of including the back of the skull as part of the wave. Let's see what she sees:

4 crests (C) - high points of the wave
3 troughs (T) - low points of the wave

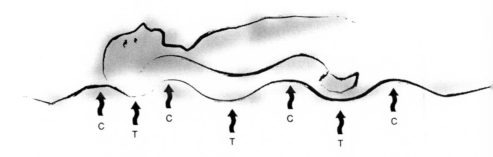

These seven extreme points on the spine wave become markers for the energetic power points we will be exploring in the next chapter. While the actual bones that form the landmarks of these fluctuations seem hard and inflexible, the energy that they host is dynamic and malleable. The apices of the curves, where the spine changes direction, represent points of focused energy. The physical bones are merely indications of the areas in which the energetic activity takes place.

Now that we can see the spine as a horizontal wave, it becomes easier to superimpose the feeling we get from the dynamic power of ocean waves onto the more dense notion we usually hold of the spine. Even in our upright, vertical posture we can sense the flow of energy, the dynamic power and life force resident in the wave of the spine. This is our first important step toward dissolving blockages. Achieving a clear, sparkling, expressive flow of life force is our goal. The spine is our instrument. We tend to see it only in its most material aspect. Not anymore.

The Energetic Spine

Let's go back to our physical bar magnet. Although you can touch the magnet itself, its magnetic field cannot be seen or felt with the ordinary senses. We can, however, determine the shape of this magnetic field with scientific instruments. These tools make visible for us the invisible energetic field around the magnet. If we could shift our focus so that the physical magnet were to blur into obscurity and we could just see the energetic imprint of the magnetic field, we would see what could be called the "energetic magnet" (as opposed to the physical magnet).

We can take the same sort of approach to the spine. We can consider the energetic field of the spine while removing our focus from the actual bones of the spine. The energetic nature of the spine, its shape and direction of force, its behavior and degree of alignment, these are the aspects that we refer to as qualities of the energetic spine. In this case, we won't be relying on the instruments of scientists to show us the nature of this energetic field. This time we turn to the perceptions of mystics for our data. Their intense and disciplined study helps us know ourselves better. It supports us in cultivating the inner garden and thereby creating a joyful life experience.

The state of alignment of the energetic spine influences many of the choices we make. In fact, it directly affects the unfolding of our whole lives. To understand how this invisible dynamo within us manifests in our lives, we must uncover certain aspects of alignment usually hidden from view. Understanding how they impact the human body and consciousness gives us unique access to personal transformation.

Think for a minute about the spine as a string of pearls. Structurally, the pearls represent the bones of the spine, and the string represents the spinal cord of the nervous system passing through each one. As long as the hole in the center of each pearl is directly aligned with the one above and the one below, the string remains free and unfettered. The pearls glide elegantly across the string accommodating to each new movement with grace and ease.

Let's think about this again, but this time, when you visualize the spine as a string of pearls, think energetically. Each pearl represents a vortex of energy information. Neither the pearls nor the string can be touched with your hand but as you look inward, you find a wealth of experience in each pearl and infinity in the string. In the Yoga of Alignment, you will be aligning these energy centers within you for the magnificent expression of your unique incarnation.

Resonance, Holograms, and You

I had a physics professor who once spiced up a boring lecture on resonance by showing us a film about "Galloping Gertie." I guess one movie is worth a thousand equations because ever since then, I've had a profound respect for the phenomenon of resonance.

"Galloping Gertie" was the nickname for the Tacoma Narrows Bridge. After catching a resonant frequency in the 40 mph wind, the bridge began waving and twisting like a ribbon. Its own undulating motion eventually tore the bridge in two.

The Tacoma Narrows Bridge ("Galloping Gertie")[2]

Photograph courtesy of Ed Elliott and The Camera Shop

Galloping Gertie performed a dramatic demonstration of resonance. When a vibration comes into an environment of what we commonly call "the same wavelength," the wave increases in strength. Although the effects of this rule didn't work out so well for Gertie, her graphic display of the principle can give us great confidence in the power of resonance.

A more fortunate example of resonance would be how magnificent your voice sounds when you sing in the shower. The sound waves, bouncing off your bathroom tiles, combine in a way that enhances your natural talent. We use the same power that occurs when waves align constructively in this system of yoga. When our thoughts and words, our desires and beliefs, our feelings and actions, are in phase with each other, we resonate with our own inner truth. Good things happen in our lives. When like minds meet, they stimulate each other. When similar energies gather, amazing things can happen.

But waves don't always align in such a way that they amplify each other. If you have ever tossed a pebble onto the still surface of a pond, you've seen that pebble generate a series of concentric rings. If you've tossed two pebbles, you've watched the two families of rings cross each other creating unique patterns of interference. Interference patterns much like these make possible the mind-boggling, three-dimensional imaging of holography. The possibilities of uniqueness in these patterns are infinite.

You too represent a unique pattern of vibration, and as we know, much of your uniqueness is coded in your DNA. Even if you share genetics with a twin, you each occupy a unique location in space. That means your eyes see from a different perspective, and that changes everything.

Most of us have our own DNA, our own face, posture, voice, and perspective. Recently we have become more and more aware of the fact that the DNA necessary for the creation of the whole body lives within each cell of that body. That means that if you have approximately 100 trillion cells, that you also have 100 trillion identical copies of the manual for building your own unique body. Your heart cells hold within their core the same information for building your brain as your brain cells do. Your liver cells know everything there is to know about making your spleen. There is no cell in the body that carries instructions exclusively for its own creation and development. Each cell contains within its nucleus what we might call a virtual version of *the whole of which it is a part.*

Holograms do the same thing. Unlike the negative of a photograph, which when cut in half would produce only half the image, the film of a hologram, when cut in pieces, still produces the whole picture. No matter how many snips and divisions you might inflict on the 2 dimensional medium, the image stays whole. Each segment of holographic film contains a virtual version of *the whole of which it is a part.*

In the case of the 2-D holographic film, this phenomenon does something extraordinary. It catapults the system up a whole dimension. It projects from a two dimensional plate a three dimensional image—something the photographic negative can't even dream of. How can a flat piece of film, containing rings of interference patterns resembling our pond ripples, produce an image that we can walk around, seeing its back and then its front? It all hinges on natural code, records of unique states of alignment.

Our bodies are similarly coded. I used to be bothered by this display of the body's apparent inefficiency. I couldn't understand why such a magnificent system would bother creating such an excess of DNA. I quickly came to understand that what scientists call the "redundancy of the genetic material" has all to do with holograms.

This phenomenon of *the whole being contained in each of the parts* boosts the holographic film up a dimension, from 2-D to 3-D. This principle also works in us. I'd like to put forth the understanding that having the whole of the blueprint of the body contained in each one of our cells has a holographic effect. It propels us into another dimension. Since we are already 3-D, it promotes us to the dimension of conscious awareness. It moves our three dimensional living body into the fourth dimension of self-awareness.

And if that is true, then what about the spine? If you can think of each of us as a cell within the greater body of humanity, then the spine wave is our nucleus. What the DNA is to the cell, the spine wave is to the body. And what the cell is to the body, you are to the world. That means that you contain within you a virtual version of *the whole of humanity of which you are a part*. From you spring all possibilities for this world. Depending on how you align your energy, your thoughts, your words, and your deeds, you create the holographic garden in which you live. You generate your world.

Within the Upanishads, sacred texts of India, this truth finds eloquent revelation:

> *He who sees all beings in the Self and the Self in all beings, he never turns away from It (the Self).*

> *He who perceives all beings as the Self, for him how can there be delusion or grief, when he sees this oneness (everywhere)? He who perceives the Self everywhere never shrinks from anything, because through his higher consciousness he feels united with all life. When a man sees God in all beings and all beings in God, and also God dwelling in his own Soul, how can he hate any living thing?*[3]

Chapter Notes

[1] From the Abraham-Hicks Workshop recording, Boca Raton, Florida 1/27/01 www.abraham-hicks.com

[2] Photograph from The Camera Shop, courtesy of Ed Elliott and The Camera Shop. On November 7th, 1940, the Tacoma Narrows Bridge tore itself in two. To see a video of the bridge waving like a ribbon, visit www.RootedintheInfinite.com. To purchase the video or DVD, visit www.camerashoptacoma.com

[3] Translated by Swami Paramananda from the original Sanskrit text. Full text can be viewed at http://www.yoga-age.com/upanishads/isha.html

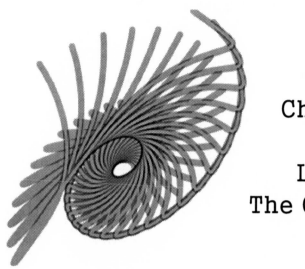

Chapter 3
Seven
Lotuses:
The Chakras

The lotus flower is known for its exquisite blossoms that brilliantly unfold in the murkiest of waters. It is completely indifferent to its muddy environment. A symbol of unconditional beauty, the lotus expresses its magnificence in spite of circumstances. Wouldn't it be nice if we could do that too? When finding ourselves in a challenging or undesirable situation, if we could rely on ourselves to act from a place of wisdom, courage, and confidence, we might seed many wonderful new realities.

All we need is to cultivate our own inner lotuses. Within the clutter and confusion of our mental field, seven bold lotuses bloom. Let's bring them into view in our lives.

The energy centers called chakras have been compared to spinning wheels, pearls on a string, and vibrating lotuses. They have been described in books, on websites, in magazines, and even on T-shirts. This chapter may be a bit of a review for you if you have already worked with the chakras, but because of our unique angle on this subject, and because of our specific goals and methods, there may be something new for you here. If you are scratching your crown chakra wondering what this is all about, this chapter is especially for you.

The Lotus Dwellers

"She is calm in a crisis." "He always sees the best in everyone." "She is like a breath of fresh air." "He turns lemons into lemonade." The people who inspire these old sayings are anything but ordinary. These people effortlessly uplift others. They inspire others by their mere presence in a room. They put you at ease and make you feel at home in your own skin. I wouldn't be surprised if you are one of these people much of the time.

These people who spread love and joy as they go are ones who knowingly or unknowingly have aligned their energetic spine. Their lotuses are in full bloom and they dwell in an outer world that matches the beauty of their inner garden. No matter what type of situation they walk into, "they come out smelling like a rose." Rather than resonating with the undesirable forces that surround them and tearing themselves apart in the process like our friend Gertie did, they set their own tone (as Abraham puts it). If others are receptive, they can become attuned to the tone of the ones whose lotuses sing.

We can always tell when we have had the good fortune to meet one of these unusual folks because we come away feeling refreshed, reconnected, and liking ourselves better. In this system, rather than seeking to meet such inspired beings, you can move toward becoming one yourself. In order to move toward this level of authentic living, we cultivate the lotuses within us known as the seven chakras.

What is a Chakra?

A chakra is an invisible part of our anatomy. Named for the wheel, it has been described as a spinning vortex of energy along the energetic spine. An area where life force pools and rotates, it is a place where you as an individual have focused access to the energy of the universe.

Mystics throughout time have perceived many different chakras, but most agree that there are seven major chakras along the spine and it is those seven centers that we are working with here. Each chakra, located at a different point along the energetic spine, provides us with a strength, a virtue, and a source of infinite potential for the brilliant unfolding of our unique gifts. Each lotus, when allowed to receive an abundant flow of life force, beautifies the inner garden and manifests many blessings in our lives.

The Seven Chakras

Our first clue that these centers of energetic activity might really exist comes from what we already know about the spine wave (Chapter 2). We saw that within the five curves of the spine wave, there were seven points of extreme high or low. These are the points where the spine changes direction. These seven power points correspond directly to the locations of the seven major chakras. If we look again at the diagram of the spine wave, we can take a tour of the chakras from bottom to top, or in the case of this diagram, from right to left. We find the chakras at the four high points and three low points of the spine wave. The words "high" and "low" imply no value judgment in this context. In fact, if you turn over on your stomach, high and low reverse themselves. So, let's call them both "turning points" or TP's for short.

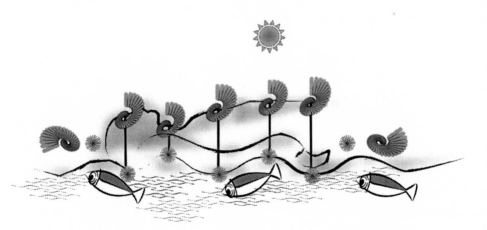

1. The bottom-most bone of the spine, the coccyx, leads to the first TP of our system. The tip of the coccyx points to the location of the first chakra, anatomically located at the perineum. It is called Muladhara in Sanskrit but is more commonly referred to in our culture as the root chakra.

2. The second chakra can be found at the spine wave's second TP. It is located at the extreme low point of the curve created by the sacrum. It projects forward to the area of the pubic bone on the front of the body. Svadhishtana in Sanskrit, the second chakra is sometimes called the sacral chakra.

3. What goes down must come up according to our system and our spine wave rises again. The third chakra, located at the crest of the lumbar curve, is called Manipura in Sanskrit and the solar plexus in common language. There is some controversy over the location of Manipura. Yogic texts mostly agree that it can be found at the level of the navel. Many new age sources place it higher, between the navel and the sternum, or breast bone (corresponding to the physical location of the solar plexus). We use the classical yogic description of the third chakra's location at the navel, while understanding that there is an energetic association between Manipura and the solar plexus.

4. As the spine wave dips back down into the back of the chest, we find Anahata or the heart chakra at the deepest part of the thoracic curve. This chakra projects forward to the center of the chest.

5. Rising again, the wave peaks in the cervical region where we find Vishuddha or the throat chakra.

6. Including the back of the skull in the wave formation, at the TP of the cranial curve, we find the point directly

behind the more famous third eye (the space between the eyebrows), Ajna chakra in Sanskrit.

7. As we follow the curve of the cranium upward, we come to the seventh and highest of the energy centers, Sahasrara or the crown chakra. Like the first chakra, the seventh is open-ended and implies the continuation of the spine wave through infinity.

Each of the chakras has numerous attributes. Since so many books have been written on this subject, I will be very brief in discussing them here as I could hardly do justice to this subject which has been handled in great depth by many experts in this field. Here I only present the attributes of the chakras that may be useful to us as we do our work in the inner garden.

The Five Elements

You're standing on the beach with the waves at your feet, the sun shining on your face, and a breeze blowing through your hair. Earth, water, fire, and air all present, the elements we experience in nature give us a strong feeling and tangible reference points for the more subtle elements we find in the chakras. These subtle elements are not like the visible, tactile, pounding water of the ocean or the wet sand embracing your feet. They are also not like the elements we study in chemistry. In fact they are not physical at all. The elements spoken of in yoga are vibrational. They permeate the body, and also, in their more subtle form, the mind. We are about to explore their relationship to consciousness and cultivate their essences in the inner garden.

Let's look at the five elements in this system. The process we are about to embark upon in this book is a journey of purification. Just as gold or oil or any other great natural resource becomes more precious to us according to its level of refinement, so our consciousness, our life itself, reveals its radiance as we refine our vibration.

In order to do this in a way that creates palpable results, we must broaden our understanding of the interface between the physical and nonphysical aspects of our nature. Body, mind, what is it all made of? How does it all stay together and what is the nature of the connection?

The tangible body, as well as the intangible mind and emotions, are composed of subtle, recognizable energies, which we call elements. You may think of yourself as your body and your mind, but your body and your mind may think of themselves as earth, water, fire, air, and ether.

The field of your individual being is an energetic composite of five basic essences, and each of the first five chakras has a particular element that presides over its territory. Because each element represents a certain vibration, it generates a color and a sound that reside in the chakra. The element gives the chakra its tone and personality. Your ability to joyfully experience and express the essence of an element harmonizes and energizes its corresponding chakra.

The Evolution of the Elements

Undifferentiated cosmic energy pours into you from above. It gradually comes into form as the subtle elements in the following order[1]:

1. Ether
2. Air
3. Fire
4. Water
5. Earth

Understanding this evolution of the subtle elements as they live right inside of you helps you break up old outmoded notions about the nature of reality. It shifts you into a much higher gear so that you can quickly move past the thought that everything is solidly fixed in its already created state. It lets you move swiftly past your densely packed belief systems and allows some light to shine into the picture. With that, change is possible. With that, there is the possibility of creating something new within a situation that previously may have seemed hopeless.

Ether

Our story begins with what some might call empty space. You can think of it as a blank canvas. It's like the stage before the play begins. It is the neutral medium in which reality takes place. It is called ether.

Ether is the subtlest of the elements. It is strictly potential energy. Because it is undifferentiated, it holds within it infinite possibility. Both energy and matter lie dormant in ether.

Whenever you focus your meditative attention on ether, it has the effect of heightening your spiritual awareness. It is not strongly tied to sensory or material concerns so its cultivation leads to spiritual gains rather than material ones. It is related to the unconscious mind and it lives vibrationally in the fifth chakra at the throat. Its seed syllable is ham. Ether's color is blackish since it has nothing in it.

When you look at a painting, although you are focused on the picture, the canvas remains silently present. The artist can always add more paint and change the picture completely. The stage holds up the play, and although you sit at the edge of your seat engrossed in the drama, the stage offers the actors the perpetual opportunity to change their lines.

Let's begin to open our awareness to the notion that, although our lives are filled with forms, relationships, tangible realities, much paint and many dramas, the infinite potentiality of ether remains ever present. It's vibration silently and perpetually offers new possibilities in every situation.

Air

Each element evolves from one more subtle than itself. It begins here. When the energy of ether begins to vibrate, it creates movement. This movement is no longer purely characteristic of ether which basically has no distinct properties at all. From the movement of ether, air is born. Air signifies freedom of movement. Wind is its nature. The vibration of ether also creates light. This light turns the blackish void of ether to the gray-blue color of the air element.

Air, like its predecessor ether, remains in an undifferentiated form. It can best be thought of as kinetic energy. It is movement itself. Like ether, it is very subtle and does not maintain a form. Therefore, meditation on the air element is not conducive to material manifestation. Air is the basis of rational thought and is beneficial for intuition and literary pursuits. Its seed syllable is yam. Its vibrational home is the heart chakra.

Now we can begin to understand that within our body, our situations, our relationships and our world, not only is there the silent blessing of ether, ever offering us brand new potential, there is more. The air element is also ever present within us. No matter how still or stagnant a situation may appear to be, it contains within its energetic makeup, the essence of movement. Again, this reassures us that nothing is stuck in its place. Change is always possible.

Fire

As air's movement becomes excessive, it heats up and creates fire. With the formation of the fire element, the freedom of motion (characteristic of air) becomes slightly constricted. Fire, although its form may be fleeting and fluid, is the first element to actually have a form. It suggests the first inkling of manifestation in the evolution of energy. (Ether and air were still unformed.)

It is made of light vibrating at a frequency that produces the color red. Fire also regulates digestion, appetite, thirst, and sleep. Its seed syllable is ram. Fire's vibrational home is in the third chakra located at the navel.

By the light of the fire, the eye sees form. The importance of this occurrence cannot be overstated because as the eye (the sense organ associated with fire) becomes aware of form, the ego is born. We will look further into the relationship between ego and the third chakra in Chapter 12.

The subtle essence of fire that is part of our natural makeup, like that of ether and air, is always available. Where ether gave us the possibility of new creation (change), and air gave us the necessary movement, fire acts as a catalyst for transformation. With each element we are further empowered to transform our current situation regardless of appearances.

Water

A decrease in motion dispels some of the heat. Eventually, the fire begins to cool down, creating water.

Water displays much less freedom of movement than air or fire. It is the first element to be confined to a definite space. With the creation of water, the energy has finally emerged as matter. Water controls the fluids of the body and has a beneficial influence on more worldly events, but because of its quickly changing form, it does not produce long lasting material effects. Its seed syllable is vam and it is visualized as white. Its vibration resides in the second chakra at the pubic bone.

The water element holds within its fluid form that which is about to be created. Correlated with the womb, it is the step before the birthing of our tangible reality. Once again, you benefit by holding an awareness of the ever-flowing water essence as it permeates your body, mind, and experience. It holds your new moment in its gestational womb and gives you an intuitive glimpse of what you are in the process of creating before it has fully taken form.

Earth

The greatest slowing of movement is manifested in the earth element where the energy achieves its lowest frequency of vibration, assuming a yellow color and acquiring the attributes of solidity, weight, and cohesion. Earth brings stability and permanence and is most beneficial for material pursuits. Its seed syllable is lam. Earth finds its vibrational home in the root chakra.

Remembering that the earth element resides within you brings a sense of stability, heightened sensory awareness, and a great appreciation of the human experience.

The Lotus Petals

The number of petals on each of the lotuses tells us how many energy channels are associated with that chakra. These channels, called nadis, are more like acupuncture meridians than like nerves although they are compared to both. We can find no physical evidence of them like we can nerves, and there are many more of them than there are meridians. Some sources report the existence of as many as 350,000 of these pathways. Others describe them more generally as "innumerable." The word nadi comes from the Sanskrit word for current of force. We have been talking about the flow of energy. The various systems of yoga describe these nadis as intricate channels that allow life force to flow through the entire body. Each petal of the lotuses tapers to a point where it extends into a nadi through which energy can flow. The number of petals on each lotus is as follows:

First chakra-4, second chakra-6, third chakra-10, fourth chakra-12, fifth chakra-16, sixth chakra-2, seventh chakra-1000 (symbolic of infinity).

	1 Root Chakra	2 Sacral Chakra	3 Solar Plexus	4 Heart Chakra	5 Throat Chakra	6 Third Eye	7 Crown Chakra
Sanskrit Name	Muladhara	Svadhishtana	Manipura	Anahata	Vishuddha	Ajna	Sahasrara
Spine Wave Location	Coccygeal Crest	Sacral Trough	Lumbar Crest	Thoracic Trough	Cervical Crest	Cranial Trough	Cranial Crest
Surface Location	Perineum	Pubic Bone	Navel	Center of Chest	Pit of Throat	Between Eyebrows	Crown of Head
Shape	Square	Crescent Moon	Inverted Triangle	Hexagonal Star of David	Circle	Circle	Beyond
Petals	4	6	10	12	16	2	1000 (Infinite)
Seed Sound	Lam	Vam	Ram	Yam	Ham	Om	
Element	Earth	Water	Fire	Air	Ether	Mind	Beyond
Sense	Smell	Taste	Sight	Touch	Hearing	Mind	Beyond
Work Organ	Anus	Sex organs, Kidney, urinary system	Feet, Legs	Hands	Vocal Chords	Mind	Beyond

Each petal also contains a Sanskrit letter that corresponds to the vibration of the nadi. The letters glow in the petals and vibrate in the chakra. These sounds, in addition to the seed syllable of the element, promote resonance in the chakra when used as a mantra in meditation.

The chart on the previous page will give you familiarity with these and other attributes of the chakras.

Inner Harvest

Aligning the physical spine yields health and vitality by allowing the proper flow of information through the nerves. Aligning the energetic spine promotes general health and vitality by allowing the proper flow of life force through the chakras. It also clears the path for our most cherished human qualities, such as love, wisdom, and courage, to shine through us. As you work with the methods of inner alignment presented in this book, your chakras receive an abundant flow of life force. Your whole being gets the opportunity to become vitalized. These energy centers within you then become active springs of healing and enlightenment.

How do we do it? We turn within and align our energy through focused attention. Our inner garden can then flourish as a result of our loving care.

Chapter Notes

[1] For more information about the evolution of the elements, consult *Tattwa Shuddhi, The Tantric Practice of Inner Purification* by Swami Satyasangananda Saraswati under the direct guidance of Swami Satyananda Saraswati, Bihar School of Yoga, India, 1984

Chapter 4

Tilling
the Soil:
Techniques

E very gardener knows the exhilarating feeling of looking out
   at the freshly tilled, lush brown earth, cleared of last season's debris and decay. Miraculously new again with every
spring, the cleared land holds the gardener's dream for the unborn
garden.

Tilling the soil of our consciousness has a similar effect. It
brings a whole new field of possibilities into view. Once the mental
ground is freshly tilled, we are granted the profound privilege of
being able to begin each moment new.

Like the earth, which gives us this amazing gift, year after year,
the fertile ground of consciousness wastes no opportunity to further our growth and advance our journey. Even the most challenging and disagreeable experiences can be composted into nourish-
ment for the inner garden. The ground offered by the earth and the
ground offered by our inner being, both turn old into new. Both
can turn the stench of what is rotting into the fragrance of spring.

All either ground asks of us is that we do a little gardening, and
the bountiful color, flavor, and nutrition will be provided. For this
we need a few simple tools. In this chapter we explore the gardening store of the mind. The shovels, rakes, and hoes that you pick

out as you shop make the job not only doable but also enjoyable. The following tools for inner gardening will be of great use as we move through this system. For now, I suggest you just read through them. Then, be prepared to return here and use the checklist you'll find later in this chapter when you begin doing the inner alignment exercises in the Practice Section. Using the information presented here will bring greater satisfaction as you move through the book.

Clearing last year's garden from view and opening the space for new flowers to grow is a process of letting go. When we let go of the rot and decay, it lets go of us. By clearing the mind of habitual conflicting thought patterns, old behaviors begin to release their hold on you. This allows you to live in closer harmony with your own true nature. You only need a few tools for this tremendously rewarding job.

Sitting

Developing good sitting posture right from the beginning establishes the necessary support to do this inner work. Although sitting would seem to be self-explanatory, the discomfort some people feel while they sit has probably cut short many a meditation session. We can do away with this potential obstacle by beginning with a comfortable, self-supporting posture.

Remember the strap I briefly wore to improve my posture? It tried (unsuccessfully) to pull back my shoulders. We won't go that route. Rather than trying to build a house from the roof down, we will first establish our foundation. The most important part of our sitting begins with how our bottom meets the chair or cushion.

Let's return for a moment to the spine wave we looked at in Chapter 2. It's helpful to remember that, as we sit up, the spine remains a wave. The alignment that we seek here creates a right angle between the center of the spine wave and the surface of the earth.

It's not just that it makes a pretty picture or appeals to our sense of order; it is that it allows us to employ gravity to our benefit.

Gravity is in the business of pulling everything in toward the center of the earth. If we dropped a plumb line from the top of the spine wave, and it went through the entire wave, that position would represent the most effortless sitting posture you could adopt for your meditation. It would mean that your structural alignment was doing as much of the work of holding you up as possible, allowing many muscle groups to relax while you sit in alignment with the center of the earth.

Here are three ways of sitting that can help you achieve physical alignment to support your inner work. See which one bests fits your body.

Cross-Legged

The full lotus position might just be the most ideal sitting posture for meditation. Unfortunately, most Westerners (myself included) can't do it, or at least not without a lot of pain. So instead of sitting that way (unless it is comfortable for you), lets look at why it is so beneficial and see how we can receive those same benefits from a modified way of sitting cross-legged. The full lotus offers three main advantages: stability, support, and energy circulation.

Stability: Because of the triangular base created by the buttocks and knees, this sitting posture is very stable. The legs are interlocked, creating a foundation that will not shift. The body becomes suggestive of a pyramid, a symbol of stability.

Support: The interlocking of the legs sets the pitch of the pelvis. With the pelvis at the proper tilt, the spine more easily balances in a straight vertical line. The goal of maintaining the spine at a right angle with the earth gets perpetual support from this stable foundation.

Energy Circulation: As energy flows through the legs, it is circulated back into the spine so there is no energy loss. The energy efficiency of this posture enhances the flow of energy in meditation.

If you want to approximate the stability, support, and energy circulation of the full lotus without the pain and discomfort, try this. Sit on a cushion on the floor. Experiment with cushions of different heights and densities until you find one that lets your spine click into alignment with gravity. With your buttocks on the edge of the cushion, leave your knees on the ground. Bend your knees so that both your heels are tucked in as close to each other as possible, resting comfortably on the ground. A thin flat cushion or folded blanket under your legs and the sitting cushion makes this a comfortable experience. If you explore, you can find many beautiful zafu and zabuton sets that will support both the structure and the aesthetics of your alignment sessions.

The sitting cushion helps stabilize your pyramid and also corrects the pitch of your pelvis to support your upright spine. Without the cushion, your lower back may tend to form a big "C" and this is best corrected before it begins. With the cushion elevating your pelvis, you are stable and supported and your legs are directing the energy back to your spine. With this sitting posture you are ready to have an enjoyable session of inner alignment with many of the benefits of the full lotus.

Seiza

If all bodies were the same, we would only need one kind of sitting posture, but if your knees and hips rebel against the cross-legged option, you might want to try the seiza position. Here you sit with your legs folded underneath you. This position provides stability, and since it elevates your pelvis, it also pitches the spine well for upright sitting. The energy is again directed back to the spine through the feet. You can use a cushion or even buy a little seiza bench that will take the weight off your legs and feet.

In a Firm Chair

I know you are already an expert at sitting on a chair, and with a little fine tuning you can turn those years of experience into a tool for meditation. If you choose to use a chair, sit at the edge of the seat so you don't make any contact with the back of the chair. A seat with a firm cushion is usually best. If the seat is too low or your legs are too long you may find your knees rise higher than your hips. This will turn your lower back into a "C" and make sitting upright a much bigger effort than it needs to be. Your search for a chair that helps you achieve the right pitch for your pelvis will bring wonderful dividends in the form of ease of concentration later on. It's worth testing a few different seats before finding the one that you decide to use on a regular basis. What you are looking for is a sense that your spine clicks into alignment with gravity and your sitting feels almost effortless. When using a chair for meditation, remember to sit at the edge of the seat with your feet flat on the floor.

Intention

Once you have your sitting worked out, it might be a good idea to ask yourself why in the world you are doing this. I know you are here and that should be good enough, but if you are a Westerner like myself, then you are probably culturally driven by action and accomplishment. Most of us will at some point find it difficult to switch gears from the busy pace of our lives to the quiet sitting of meditation. In fact, there may even be days when the little voice in your head will whisper, "What good can possibly come from sitting and doing nothing?" At those moments, it will be very handy to already know the answer. Because if you try to figure out your intention at that moment, it may seem like your whole purpose in life is to pay your bills, or watch TV, or forage for a snack.

Why *are* we doing this? What we all have in common here is that we want a beautiful inner garden, but I may want to grow a field of watermelons while you may want a trellis of roses. As you plan your inner garden, choose your seeds with care because, as ancient wisdom tells us, "As you sow, so shall you reap." There is also a wise expression that warns us not to wish too hard for what we want because we might just get it. The bottom line is this: check your intention. We will find most intentions gravitate toward one of three points on the compass: spiritual awareness, healing, and joyful manifestation.

Spiritual Awareness

The first category is spiritual and this is probably the most frequent intention that brings people to meditation. With this intention, you may be seeking to bring your individual awareness into closer harmony with God. You may want to bring an experience of divine love and wisdom into your daily life.

Even with the loftiest of intentions, in the course of the day, you still may find yourself in the heat of an argument, or fuming with unexpressed anger. You may fall into the mire of depression, or succumb to the grip of anxiety. At any of those moments you can shift your state into greater alignment. Your inner alignment will strengthen your ability to "set your own tone" as Abraham says. It amplifies the perspective of your transcendent Self while dissolving the more troublesome distortions created by patterns of conflicting energy.

In those difficult moments, you can turn to your inner practice to bring divine light into your material existence. When you have the time to sit quietly without distractions, you can set an intention to align yourself with your true nature. This opens you to all you consider to be good.

Healing

More and more people are turning to meditation for the purpose of healing. If you have a health problem that has brought you to this book, you probably have a strong desire to do what you can to get healthy again. The pain and anxiety that often accompany illness can be great motivators, but they offer a subtle challenge that I'd like to point out here.

When people get sick, they usually focus on *not wanting to be sick* more than they focus on *wanting to be healthy*. It makes perfect sense, but intention always works *for* something, never *against* anything. So if you find yourself stating your intention in the negative, then your first task will be to dig deeper to find a true intention. Examples of some negative statements masquerading as intentions are as follows:

> I don't want this illness.
> I want to stop smoking.
> I want this pain to end.

These desires spring from reactions to unwanted circumstances but they have not yet formed into positive intentions. To help them along, you must look deeper into your heart. What brightens your spirit? What powers your engines? What puts a smile on your face? What offers a little relief? Whatever uplifts you is closer to your true intention than the idea of ridding yourself of what is unwanted. It might help to integrate your intention to heal with intentions that fall into the other two categories (spiritual and joyful manifestation).

Joyful Manifestation

Here we are turning our attention to the realms of work, school, relationships, finances, and all the manifestations of the outer, material world. We can describe success as joy in the journey. What does your inner state of alignment have to do with success? More than you might imagine.

Acquisitions in the material world and the attachments that form in relationships have gotten a very bad rap in most spiritual traditions. Here, rather than attempting to renounce these desires, we will instead purify, harmonize, and embrace them. If you have goals and ambitions regarding your work, inner alignment offers an opportunity to turn yourself into the person who can be joyful when your goals are achieved.

One person fails because he doesn't achieve what he wants and he feels defeated. Another will reach his goal but will not be happy when he gets there. Both have "failed" because they lost touch with their joy. Fortunately, as Abraham tells us, "You can't get it wrong and you never get it done." Both fellows have a brand new slant in this moment. So nothing is lost. Let's look at what happened with them.

They both forgot to align their intention with their heart's desire before taking action. The first fellow's lack of alignment sabotaged his results. The second man's failure to align himself first left him empty and disappointed with his "win." Through his great skill, he accurately hit the bull's-eye, but on the wrong target.

You can see how the question of alignment can apply to everything from applying for a job, to getting married, to recovering from a trauma, to just about anything. When you want any venture to be successful, align your energy first. Purify your intention so that you are sure to hit the target, the right target. Inner alignment is to success what aim is to accuracy.

No matter in which of the three categories you find your intention (and it may change from session to session) let the aim of your intention be to align yourself on that subject. Then let it go. You will not be thinking about that subject in the meditation nor will you be making plans for its fulfillment. Like an arrow that you aim and release, once your intention is launched, you trust your aim and wait to see how it turns out. We have no idea how long it will take or how the fulfillment of our desire will come to us. Our only task is to bring ourselves into alignment with that which we truly desire with every fiber of our being. If you cannot feel whole in your commitment to an intention, then it is not in harmony with your heart's desire. Back to the drawing board.

There is one more test of a true intention that is worth mentioning here. If the fulfillment of your intention will hurt you or cause harm to anyone else, it is not a true intention. A true intention acts through wisdom on the heart's desire and benefits everyone touched by its fulfillment.

Concentration

We are in the habit of calling upon concentration when we have a difficult task to accomplish. We tend to develop this skill for intellectual pursuits. We associate concentration with complexity and mental difficulty. Here, we engage in a different kind of concentration. The yogic practice of concentration is the exact opposite of engaging in intellectual complexity. It is based on simplicity and it promotes ease of mind.

By focusing the energy of the entire field of consciousness on a single point, we achieve what is known as dharana, or concentration. With the Yoga of Alignment, you will practice a specific form of concentration that prepares you energetically for meditation. If you already have a meditation practice, adding the YOFA™ exercises to your routine before your meditation session can get you to meditate more often, more regularly, and more deeply.

The sun's rays concentrated through a lens can start a fire. The concentrated power of the steam engine can move tons of cargo. Swami Sivananda has pointed out these examples of concentration to help us appreciate the power of the untapped potential that sits diffused in our undisciplined minds.

Once we focus the mind through concentration, we open the way for the arrival of that which we have already intended: spiritual awareness, healing, and joyful manifestation. Through concentration we till the mental field and release the clutter of the weeds and old rotten thought-forms that litter the inner garden. Once the field of our consciousness is tilled, we can sow the seeds of our heart's true desires. We can open to a greater experience of the presence of God. We can better express ourselves physically. We can manifest a life of kind and loving relationships, fulfilling work, an abundance of beautiful things, and joy in the experience of it all.

How do we do it? How do we develop the degree of concentration that will prepare the ground for our inner garden? That's what this book is all about. In the alignment processes that appear in the Practice Section, you will have many opportunities to gather your mind to one point. As intruding thoughts present themselves, simply bring your mind back to the point of focus. It is a relaxed process and since we know that extraneous thoughts will arise in abundance, there is no reason to ever feel you are doing it "wrong" or that you are "not good at it."

The object of concentration may vary but the activity is always the same. It is keeping the mind steady on an external object or an internal point. Sri Swami Satchidananda calls it, "the binding of the mind to one place, object or idea." Some use a visual image as a focusing tool, some use sound, words, breath, sensations, or thoughts. In all cases, the mind is gently gathered to that one object of concentration.

In this system we will be sensing points in our energetic body, using the physical body as our frame of reference. These points will serve all three categories of intention previously mentioned: spiritual awareness, health, and joyful manifestation. The rest of the book is dedicated to the exposition of this system. Two other objects of concentration may be used in harmony with the main body of this work. They are breath and mantra.

Have you ever changed a baby's diaper? The baby may twist and squirm, cry and try to flip over. Back when I was trying to get the hang of changing diapers, a dear friend told me to give the baby a rattle to hold while I was doing the messy work. Amazing! It worked. I like to think of the object of concentration as the rattle you give to your squirming, restless mind. Content with its toy, the mind becomes calm and relaxed while you clean up your vibration.

Meditation

If everything I just described is concentration, then what is meditation? The term *meditation* is commonly used to describe many different aspects of inner practice. In yoga, however, meditation specifically refers to the evolved and purified form of concentration. Sri Swami Satchidananda says, "Concentration is the beginning of meditation; meditation is the culmination of concentration. They are more or less inseparable."[1]

Once your concentration is uninterrupted, like "the continuous flow of oil from one vessel to another" or the "flow of water in a river,"[2] once your mind rests steadily on your object of concentration, that state is called meditation. I use the terms *concentration, inner alignment,* and *meditation* somewhat interchangeably in this book. One is simply the fulfillment of the other, but, to be truly accurate with our language, I would say that this system outlines a *concentration* practice of *inner alignment* that prepares us for *meditation*.

Your mind takes on the shape of that which you think about. "As a man thinketh in his heart so is he."[3] Although you use the object of your meditation as a tool to focus the mind, and theoretically you could use anything for this purpose, we choose these objects very carefully. They have a tremendous influence on the inner garden. If you use something as your object of concentration that is resonant with your intention, you advance rapidly. As your concentration evolves into meditation, you steep yourself in the qualities of your object of concentration. Those same qualities then emanate from your being and attract more of the same.

Paramahansa Yogananda says, "Meditation is that special form of concentration in which the attention has been liberated from restlessness and is focused on God. Meditation, therefore, is concentration used to know God."[4]

Breathing

The breath is nature's own wave of life force that rhythmically moves through us. An excellent object of concentration, many schools of meditation utilize this naturally occurring movement as a point of focus. While some schools of yoga aim at controlling the breath, here we seek to allow it.

Before doing any of the inner alignment exercises suggested in this book, I recommend that you take a few moments after arranging your sitting and setting your intention, to do some conscious breathing. This means you use the wave of your breath as your object of concentration. Nothing else exists for you. Close your eyes and feel your breath. Without placing any judgment on it, notice how it feels. Let it flow in and out at its own pace and let it seek its own depth. Wait patiently for the inhalation to follow the exhalation on its own. Give your breath total freedom to be however it wants to be. As your mind wanders, simply bring it back to the feeling of the breath wave. Sense its rising and falling as a continuous stream. Feel your spine wave and your breath wave merging into the same shape and let that shape fill you. Feel the autonomy of the life force that breathes through you without your conscious effort.

Once you have explored this system of inner alignment, you may find it a valuable practice to help you center yourself before beginning more traditional sessions of breath-based styles of meditation.

Mantra

"Just as soap cleanses the cloth of its impurities, so also, Mantra is a spiritual soap cleansing the mind. Just as fire cleanses gold of its impurities, so also, Mantra cleanses the mind of its impurities." Swami Sivananda tells us of the purifying power of mantra as an object of concentration. Mantra, the repetition of a sound, word, or group of words, can increase one's focus and summon tremendous spiritual energy. Mantra harmonizes the whole of our being producing peace, freedom, and bliss.

Traditionally, mantras were names for God and contained the vibration of deities. They originated from Self-realized beings who achieved liberation through the mantra and passed it on. But all sounds are vibrating and the simple use of our own English words such as *love, beauty,* and *freedom* can be repeated with great benefit. Like the smooth rattle we give to the agitated baby, the mantra of love is safe and soothing.

In the chapters that follow, as we explore different parts of our energetic anatomy, you may find it useful to use a mantra in your meditation. If your mind is particularly noisy, repeating the mantra out loud helps displace the mental chatter and absorb the conscious mind in the wave of the mantra. As the mind becomes resonant with the mantra, you can move to a silent repetition of the selected word or words.

Putting it All Together

By learning the techniques of concentration, we gather our tools and head into the inner garden. Good shoes that keep you dry in the mud and protect your feet from rocks and thorns make sense in the outer garden. They protect you from impediments that might slow you down or halt your work all together. A balanced and comfortable sitting posture does the same for the inner gardener. It allows your body to support you in maintaining your chosen focus.

Setting your intention bridges your thought with your action. It links your heart's desire with your meditation, and magnetizes to you the desired beneficial outcome.

Concentration is the main activity and leads to meditation. By choosing one thing with which to fill the whole mind, you quiet the mind and open to the brilliant unfolding of your life in harmony with that focus.

Focusing on the breath leads you through the doorway into the meditative process. It begins the withdrawal of your attention from the outer world and gently turns your awareness inward. It attunes you to your inner rhythm and helps you release the influence of vibrations that you may have taken on unknowingly in your daily life.

The use of a mantra, a word or group of words or sounds, harmonizes the mind and brings peace and freedom.

These simple tools, when applied to the field of consciousness, prepare the ground for the fruition of your most heart-felt desires.

Chapter Notes

[1] Sri Swami Satchidananda, Integral Yoga: *The Yoga Sutras of Patanjali* (Yogaville, Virginia: Integral Yoga Publications, 1984) page 201

[2] Swami Sivananda, *Concentration and Meditation* (India: The Divine Life Society, 1994) page 61

[3] James Allen reminds us of this in his book by this title. You can download the ebook version of *As a Man Thinketh* at www.RootedintheInfinite.com

[4] Paramahansa Yogananda, *Inner Peace* (Los Angeles California: Self-Realization Fellowship, 1999) page 29

Premeditation Checklist

In the Practice Section, you will find numerous methods of alignment. Use this simple checklist to prepare yourself energetically before beginning the specific meditation exercises. It will assist you in achieving a deeply meditative state with ease.

1. Sitting

   ☐ Make sure you are comfortable.
   ☐ Sit at the edge of your seat or cushion.
   ☐ Keep your spine upright and feel it click into alignment with gravity.

2. Intention

   ☐ Set your intention and check that your whole being is resonant with that intention.
   ☐ Envision your intention emitting light in all directions, having a beneficial influence on all touched by its fulfillment.
   ☐ Release the intention. Let it go. It does not require continued thought.

3. Breathing

   ☐ Begin concentration by putting your full attention on your breath.
   ☐ Allow your breath its own pace and depth.
   ☐ Let your breath wave merge with your spine wave.
   ☐ Feel the autonomy of your breath.

Chapter 5
Planning the
Garden:
X-Y-Z

You can feel the difference between flowing and stagnant energy within you. One feels like joy, the other feels like depression. One feels like vitality, the other feels like fatigue. Energy flows through specific pathways like rivers in your body and many of them have been mapped. The meridians outlined in acupuncture, the nadis of yoga, and the branching of the peripheral nervous system addressed by the chiropractic adjustment all describe complex energy networks within the body. YOFA™ brings to light a much simpler map. It overlaps with these other systems but steers clear of their complexity and relies mostly on intuition.

In order to experience the joy and vitality of flowing energy, your channels must be clear. We look to achieve this through a process of alignment. This system assists you in aligning your individual consciousness with your Inner Being, also called your Higher Self, Soul, or Atman. Once you begin this process of alignment, you start reaping the benefits of a more vital life experience right away.

The expansive consciousness within you, which goes by many names, transcends your individual mind or ego. It exceeds the perspective offered by your physical senses. By aligning your individual awareness with the transcendent aspect of yourself, you allow divine love, joy, and wisdom to flow through you. You transcend the limits argued by your body.

Your body convinces you of your separateness. You have no trouble telling the difference between you and me because you live in your body and I live in mine. We live in this three dimensional, physical universe, each moving in our own separate frame. But the body is more than just a way to move around. It is a language, a code that can be deciphered. Within the wisdom of the body lies the secret of its own transcendence. The body in which we each reside holds the key to our own enlightenment. Through the limits of your human form you can discover your deep connection to the Infinite.

XYZ

Your body is more than it seems. It maintains a metaphysical correspondence with the three-dimensional world all around you. In this world, the three dimensions are obvious. Width represents the horizontal, side-to-side dimension. Height represents the vertical, up-down direction. Depth measures the horizontal, front-to-back distance. If we change the words *width, height,* and *depth* to *X (width), Y (height)* and *Z (depth)*, we have all the tools we need to begin to understand the sacred architecture of the body. Now, we can begin to unmask these three dimensions and discover their metaphysical contribution to our day-to-day experience.

As legend has it, this simple way of communicating about space came about one sleepless night when French philosopher René Descartes amused himself by watching a fly on his wall. He saw that he could describe the fly's location relative to the corner of the room if he used the three lines that met at the corner of the ceiling as his map. The Cartesian coordinate system, a staple of mathematics, was born that night. We will now take these same X,

Y, and Z-axes and apply them to the inner alignment we seek. I'm happy to report that our method is based on intuition and requires no calculations. Our new language will reduce the body to three lines of direction. If you can count to three, your math skills are in gear for this simple course in X, Y, Z. Throughout this system, I talk about the body in terms of these axes.

Within the sacred architecture of the body, we find endless messages that illuminate how we are woven seamlessly into the fabric of the 3-D universe. Like ladders, handrails, or for the younger at heart, monkey bars, these axes offer us structure, support, and a frame of reference in which we can live, work, and play.

Like a Fish in Water

We tend to live unquestioningly in this perfectly fitting human body. We hardly think twice about it. We get much more intrigued by the details of losing or gaining weight, styling hair, or wrapping ourselves in colorful fabrics. All these wonderful, creative impulses to fashion the body rest on our clear knowing of the human form, but it is not the kind of knowing that probes deeply into the meaning of a thing. It is more like the way a fish knows water. We live in our bodies somewhat unconsciously.

You are about to change all that. You are about to awaken in a way that might change you forever. Yes, you are like a fish in water. Or even better stated, you are like a wave in the ocean. You are made of the same stuff that you live in. You are a hugely detailed embellishment of the X, Y and Z-axes, solidified into form.

Since you are a human being, you possess a personal version of each of these three axes. You carry these around with you everywhere you go. Each axis expresses itself in your body. When you apply the notion of these three axes to your body while you meditate, something wonderful happens. Your mind quiets down and your consciousness expands. To the degree that you bring this inner grid into your conscious awareness, you gain access to infinite potential. By aligning yourself from within, you begin a journey of mastery. Let's look at each axis in more detail.

Moving Forward

Your face is on the front of your head and your feet point in the same direction as your face. Your face and your feet define forward and backward for you. The rest of your anatomy falls into place from those two definitive marks. Your knees and hips bend the way they do to accommodate your feet in their desire to move you forward. Forward means the direction of your face. The partnership between your face and your feet must never be underestimated. It defines your Z-axis.

Trees and flowers don't have a Z-axis. No face, no feet, no forward, no backward. You can draw a circle all around an oak tree and no part of that circle has special meaning. Each oak tree will express differently within its own circle of growth.

Not us. We have a front and a back. I cannot stress this point enough. Why? Because we are like fish in water and our Z-axis tends to be invisible to us. We take it for granted. But look around at everyone you know and every stranger on the street. Look at the back of everyone's head. No face! And how about yourself? You cannot see the back of your own head. Do you begin to get a sense of the personality of the Z-axis? It is designed for movement forward and we are just one of its many expressions. If you really want to see some of the Z-axis' great artwork, look at the cheetah or any of the four-legged speed-based life forms. Their spines hug the Z-axis and forward they go.

So here we are, 6 billion or so human beings with faces and feet, all moving forward on the earth. And yet, we are all going in different directions. That's because, here on earth, the Z-axis is a personal axis. For us, the earth is a big open space and we can point our Z-axis in any direction we like. We each define forward movement for ourselves. We have complete freedom of Z. When we discover the mystical nature of the Z-axis later on, this freedom will reveal itself as a true treasure.

We inscribe our human Z-axis on the earth with every one of our roads, highways, railroad tracks, and bridges. All paths bear the signature of the Z-axis, as do most vehicles. We roll out the red carpet for those we love and respect to show honor for their Z-axis. Your outstretched hand, ready to shake the hand of your friend, links your Z-axis with his. Your forward pointing fist at the end of your rigid arm in a straight punch shoots your Z-axis energy ahead of you. The Z-axis also lives in a more abstract realm. Your line of vision invisibly marks the Z-axis ahead of you. Your footprints leave a trail of Z behind you. If you look at the letter Z as a figure in profile, you will see that it points backward and forward to ever remind us of its directional force.

The Up-Force

In the same way that we express the Z-axis in our forward facing human body, we also express the Y-axis in our human anatomy. We all grow our head on top and our feet on the bottom. Although we do have the freedom to stand on our heads if we like, we can't move our Y-axis around as easily as we did our Z-axis. That's partly because the vertical Y-axis has a greater agenda than our human anatomy. Unlike the forward-backward Z-axis, which was a personal axis, the up-down Y-axis has an earth-wide reality. This axis expresses itself as gravity. As long as we live on our native earth, *up* means toward the sky, away from the earth, against gravity. And *up* has always intrigued us. To fly has been the human preoccupation, probably since we grew our first set of earth-bound legs. I'm sure I wasn't the only little kid jumping off the picnic table in the backyard, convinced I could fly. We aspire upward. We aspire to rise spiritually and we often depict God as a presence above. If we had no gravity, what could possibly get our attention as passionately as the gravitational down-force that causes us to seek "up"?

Up is the same to the oak tree, the cheetah, and to us. We all merge in the earth-wide Y-axis consciousness. As reliable as the downward force of gravity may be, in the Y-axis we find an equal and opposite force that elevates the spirit. That up-lifting force resides within the vertical Y-axis and we human beings have the good fortune to be aligned with that most precious opportunity.

The letter Y even looks like a standing person with arms up stretched for maximum height. The Y-axis lives in us most boldly in our standing frame, but we have many anatomical echoes of the Y-axis within us. Our standing legs, hanging arms, our fingers, even the vertical dimension of our nose hums the tune of the Y-axis in the body. More subtly, the space between the legs, the space between the fingers, and all other vertical empty spaces resonate with the universal vertical Y-axis. Within the body, we can find a vertical space between the lungs, a vertical suture in the forehead, and the vertical trachea, aorta, and other significant functional structures. But none of these Y-axis representatives can hold a candle to our main, vertical anatomical core: the spine.

To call someone spineless is to insult that person. The reason for that is reflected in most healing arts. Just about every energy-based system boldly acknowledges the dominance of the central vertical flow of energy in the body. The spine, visible and physical, solidifies the Y-axis within us. We may not be able to see the governing vessel meridian of acupuncture that traces the spine, or touch sushumna nadi of yoga that flows through the center of the spine, but the spinal bones themselves leave nothing to the imagination. The spine is our springboard into the inner dimensions of the Y-axis. Here, the aspects of our body, mind, and emotions that would succumb to the down-force of gravity, meet the Y-axis up-force that effortlessly lifts us to the heights of human experience.

Balance

If you look at yourself in the mirror, you will probably find one shoulder higher than the other. Your left shoulder will be higher if you are right handed and your right shoulder will be higher if you are left handed. We are filled with visible and invisible asymmetries. With your liver on the right and your heart on the left, your body still miraculously manifests sublime balance.

Those asymmetries are the exceptions. Now let's look at the rule. To the naked eye, our right-left symmetry makes a marked impression. We are far more symmetrical than not, and there is tremendous power in this.

The secret ingredient that puts the final touch on our human form of expression comes through the genius of the side-to-side X-axis. Our right and left sides supply near mirror images of each other. That's something we have not seen in either of the other two axes. The X-axis contributes symmetry and balance to the formula for being human. That means one leg on each side, two feet on the earth.

The symmetry of your body's X-axis makes you a *two*-based being. Most people have two eyes, two ears, two arms, two legs, two lungs, two kidneys; the list goes on and on. Seeing through two eyes gives depth to your vision. Hearing with two ears helps you place the source of the sound in space. Any structure or organ that you have two of, one on the right and one on the left, adds to the X-axis component of your consciousness. It expands your sense of aliveness. It increases your personal presence in the here and now. When we delve more deeply into the nature of the here and now in Section Two, this fact will become more evident.

How does symmetry add power? Like the inexplicable thrill we get watching synchronized swimming or the power expressed by the synchronized march of an army, simultaneity increases our experience of the now. Anywhere that we have two of anything along the X-axis, we get simultaneous feelings of the *now* in stereo.

It heightens our awareness, adds dimension, and brings depth and richness to our experience. It spreads the *now* across our human feeling of being alive.

If you ever have seen the sunset over the ocean you know the brilliance of the X-axis. One straight line from left to right, glorified by color, the horizon sings the praises of the earth's X-axis. We utilize the dimension of width in our countertops, our steps, and our benches. In the body you see the X-axis in the line of the closed mouth, the shelf of the shoulders, the coronal suture that crosses the top of the head like a headband, and in the organ of the pancreas. The shape of the written letter X helps us understand how the X-axis functions in the body, but let's save that explanation for later (Chapter 10).

From Three to Infinity

Put these three dimensions, X, Y, and Z, into a test tube and watch the whole physical universe, as we know it, materialize before your eyes. Every angle, curve, and plane, every object, living or not, every beast, from amoeba to zebra (that includes us), takes physical form as these three dimensions create the frame of our reality.

In the Yoga of Alignment we will not be measuring these dimensions like the mathematicians. Put your rulers and protractors back in your pencil case! Rather, we are sensing the axes as they live inside of us. Once you close your eyes and turn your attention inward, a world as vast as the night sky presents its inner constellations. This is where we are headed. Out into inner space. No rocket, no puffy suit, no Tang. Just a nice soft cushion and a well balanced sitting posture.

What happens to your perception of your body when you close your eyes and stay still? The body, as you know it, becomes a distant memory. We are accustomed to defining our reality largely by our vision. "Seeing is believing." When you close your eyes a whole different body presents itself to your awareness. For a long time, through both art and science, we have been looking at bodies in order to know and understand them. That's a hard habit to break. Let's start now.

Artists love the subject of the human form. If you are an artist, you may have spent countless hours trying to capture the subtleties of its curves, its turns, and its fluid dynamism. The human body poses the greatest challenge and develops unparalleled skill in the artist. Paintings and sculptures of the human body fill our museums, and those of us who don't create them make pilgrimages to see them.

Scientists, on the other hand, marvel at the intricacies of the body's functioning and strive to mimic its genius. If you are a scientist, you may have spent your lifetime trying to unravel even a tiny facet of the incomprehensible intelligence of the human body. Those of us who don't engage in this study come to you for help when we need it. Fortunes are spent to acquire the knowledge you possess.

But here, with a new intention, we now set aside the outer perception of the body for a little while. We turn our attention inward in order to establish a more harmonious relationship with the Self. In this inner exploration, we set in motion a tuning process. As we align the waves of our individual identity with those of our more expansive Inner Being or transcendent Self, something wonderful happens. We augment our talents and abilities, our joy, and our wisdom. When we later choose to re-engage with the outer world, with senses heightened, abilities sharpened, mind in focus, we find life to be a more fulfilling journey.

From our inner perception, the body appears to be quite different from the artist's rendition or the scientist's diagram. Blackened space, occasional flashing lights, and an abstract sense of position replace the delicate contours that flowed from the artist's paintbrush or the detailed figures in the scientist's texts. When we close our eyes, we become more aware of direction than form. We can easily sense left and right, up and down, forward and backward. These directions become the anatomy of our inner world, and for the sake of simplicity, we call them X, Y, and Z.

Since these axes live in the realm of thought, they cannot be touched. Their presence in our consciousness gives us a magnetic orientation. They act as a compass within our own field of being. When we close our eyes and go deeply within, the distinction between mind and body dissolves and we become directly intimate with the field of life we identify as self. Within that field, the X, Y, and Z-axes offer us a map. That map directs us to dimensions of healing, self-knowledge, and self-expression beyond the ordinary.

In the physical garden, we easily map out which row will get the green beans and which will get the tomato plants. How will we organize the inner garden? In three intersecting rows, called X, Y, and Z. The inner garden now waits for our loving care.

Section II
Rooted in the
Infinite:
Creation

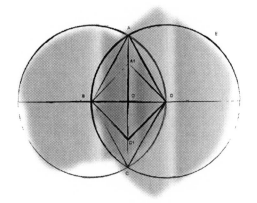

Chapter 6

Locating

Your Root

I f strong winds uproot one of the vital tomato plants in the garden, the plant will wither quickly. But if that plant can re-establish its root and reconnect with its supply, it will thrive. You and I are not so different. When we learn to establish a strong and vital root, several wonderful changes occur in our lives.

A deep and strong root uplifts you. It improves your posture, increases your energy, and raises your spirits. Along with this uplifting surge of energy comes a flood of unrealized potential ready to pour through you into magnificent expression. All your senses become enlivened. Food tastes better, music sounds sweeter, and inspiration comes more frequently when a well-established root feeds your system from its vital connection with the Infinite.

So where is this wonderful root of ours and how do we make it strong? Unlike the plant whose physical root keeps it bolted to the earth, stable and steady in one spot, our invisible root allows us to move around while still maintaining a connection with our Source. Since we have no physical evidence of this root, its existence is not widely acknowledged.

Hidden in the ancient mystical teachings of certain esoteric branches of yoga, in the past, this knowledge was only available to the select few who made enlightenment through this path their life's mission. Only in the last century has this wealth of information become available to the Western seeker[1]. It didn't take long before there was an explosion of interest in the entire chakra system. Many people today use the image of a plant-like root in guided meditation to feel grounded and connected to the earth, but the root chakra contains additional untapped resources. We will explore its hidden treasures in this section. By understanding the unique nature of the human energetic root, as distinct from that of the plant, a world of wonderful possibilities can now become realities.

In order to fully grasp the magnitude of our energetic root's potential, we must first understand its role in the creative process. The first chakra represents an ongoing font of creation. If we want to claim the wealth of this chakra's inner potential, we must dispense with the notion that we, as individual human beings, are "done" being created. We must release the idea that we were born way back when, and now the birthing process is over. As difficult as it might be to uproot this common way of thinking about life, it is of tremendous advantage to do so. In reality, a never-ending flow of creation streams though us. We birth each instant of *now* that we experience. Each *now* rises up through our consciousness via the birth canal of the first chakra.

Where is it?

The location of the root chakra causes many to overlook its importance. We don't often speak of the area known anatomically as the perineum. In fact, this small area located between the genitals and the anus (the site of the root chakra) receives no attention in a typical spiritual conversation. But just as a hen sits on her egg keeping it well concealed beneath her, we keep our first chakra tucked inconspicuously underneath our torso, well hidden from everyone, including ourselves.

If the subject leaves you feeling a little uncomfortable, don't be concerned. You're probably not alone. When we consider the significance of this location later on, you may begin to realize that wherever you sit, you are perfectly poised on a sacred point of connection with the Infinite. Once this new appreciation awakens, any discomfort with this chakra's location probably will disappear.

Since your root is not physical, its anatomical landmark can be misleading. We begin to bridge the gap between the physical location and the actual energy vortex of the chakra by focusing on the X, Y, and Z-axes as they pass through the root chakra. Finding your root does not mean locating it on your body. It means finding it in your consciousness. If you want to start now, you can turn to the Practice Section. If you'd rather keep reading for now, you can shift to the exercises later.

We are about to begin bridging the gap between your physical understanding and your energetic experience. We'll do this by entering more deeply into an understanding of the X, Y, and Z-axes. When you begin exploring the meditations in the Practice Section, you'll get to apply the notion of these axes to your own body as you locate the root chakra experientially.

Our three-dimensional world is not always what it appears to be and we are about to step behind the curtain of some of its illusions. With the X, Y, and Z-axes acting as ambassadors for the three dimensions in which we live (width, height, and depth respectively), we will now spend time with each one until its mystery has been revealed. With profound respect for the deeply sacred nature of this most fundamental chakra, let's continue our journey inward.

See Session One of the Practice Section for the experiential exercises that correspond to this chapter.

Chapter Notes

---

[1] The first edition of Sir John Woodroffe's *The Serpent Power* was published in 1918.

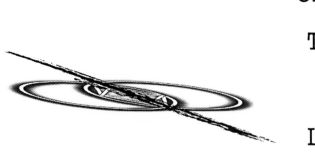

Chapter 7
The Root
of Time:
Locating
The Now

We have been told that "time is an illusion." We have been taught "time management." At times, we say that we have "wasted time," "made the most of our time," and even "bought time." Now, in the Yoga of Alignment, we visit the notion of time from a different perspective. From a new vantage point, we can transform our experience of the passing of time.

By bringing into focus the little known relationship between time and the root chakra, you can actually make your time *last longer*. You can slow down time to fit more into your day with greater ease. You can overcome fears about the future and release resentments and regrets about the past. In order to understand how all this can be possible, we begin by simply focusing our attention on the Z-axis as it passes through the root chakra.

Consider the possibility that the forward-flowing Z-axis embodies time. If that does not intuitively ring true for you just yet, the rest of this chapter maps out this concept in several different ways. If you see the correlation immediately, you are well on your way to reaping one of the main benefits of the Z-axis: joyful manifestation. Loving relationships, fulfilling work, joyful play, and material abundance are just some of the amazing manifestations created by the alignment of the Z-axis of your root chakra.

In Session One of the Practice Section, you identify the little piece of the Z-axis that passes through the root chakra marked by the front and back boundaries of the pelvis. The Z-axis also extends infinitely in front of you and behind you. Just as your car occupies a small section of the road, your body occupies a small section of the infinite forward and backward expanse of your Z-axis. Although your invisible Z-axis may seem a bit abstract, as you begin to acknowledge its presence, you will see more and more evidence of it all around you.

It's easy to spot projections of the human Z-axis on the outer world. We like to pave the Z-axis ahead of us. In the fields and jungles of omnidirectional nature, we like to establish our paths by marking our Z-axis on the earth. We share a physical Z-axis as we travel together on our highways. Our cities give us many pre-paved Z's to choose from as we decide how to get where we are going. Whether in its physical imprint as a road, or in its non-physical aspect as our personal experience of time, the Z-axis is all about getting somewhere. It's about movement forward. That is its raison d'être.

The human desire to move forward along the Z-axis is as old as the human race and as perpetual as time itself. We unconsciously merge with time through the vehicle of our Z-axis. Although we cannot see time, we can see the road ahead of us and we can clock our speed. Your personal Z-axis delineates your unique timeline. It belongs to no one else but you. It unfolds your field of potential creation, making manifest each new *now* as it goes. Time moves you, carrying you forward like the current in a stream. As you stand, always facing forward on your personal Z-axis, you embody the intention of time.

Because of its relationship with time, the Z-axis can always tell you where you stand regarding past, present, and future. The limb of the Z-axis extending toward the front of the body moves you toward the future. The back limb points to the past. The center point of the chakra, where all three axes intersect, marks the eternal present moment—every instant of *now*. This is where you will always find yourself.

The Human Anatomy of Time

Now our seemingly "unholy" landmarks, the genitals and the anus, start to make some sense. We can understand the genitals as movement forward, toward the future. Their location, front of center, is no accident. They function as Z-axis landmarks in two capacities. First, as sexual organs, they move us toward our desire. The genitals act as our engine of attraction and steer us toward our future. Second, as reproductive organs they give us offspring allowing us to feel that we live beyond our personal future. Reproduction dramatizes the constant forward push, the urge to move ahead along the Z-axis.

The less popular anus, by its location behind the center point, indicates the past. We don't usually like talking about this part of our anatomy or physiology, but its energetic counterpart, the past, certainly occupies much of our conversation. So let's consider it for just a brief moment here. The anus discards what has been used and is no longer of value to the body. We eat food (which enters from front of the center line), we extract all the value we can from it, and we excrete the remains. The wisdom of the body tells us that at this point, this material belongs behind us. With that excretion in our past, we look forward to the next meal in our future. In fact, the root chakra's sense organ, the nose, also points forward sniffing out our new desire.

The Z-axis not only speaks to us of past and future but of life and death. The reproductive organs, situated front of center, begin the next generation of life. The male's sperm contributes its Z-axis to the female's omnidirectional ovum. The sperm has only one significant axis reflecting its one significant intention. It is a Z-axis be-ing. It swims forward in the name of reproduction. Both the male genitals and the male seed cells reflect the life-affirming message of the Z-axis in form and function.

The backward pointing half of the Z-axis clearly leaves behind, via excretion, what has been used and is now "dead." The track of our Z-axis lures us forward and trips us when we try to back up. The calling of the Z-axis is to life.

We have no trouble at all knowing which is our front and which is our back. The human body has a very clearly marked Z-axis. If the human body were like the egg, it would have no personal Z-axis and the concept of forward and backward would have no meaning. There would be no landmarks to distinguish them. That would give us a completely different relationship with time from the one we have, but that is definitely not the case. Human beings are anatomically organized so that our face points forward. From there, everything, from the direction of our toes, to the course of our goals and aspirations, falls into place.

Understanding the mystical link between the body's direction-ality and the unfolding of our personal timeline puts the key to a bright future in your hand. The direction of your nose is the direc-tion of your focus. As you choose your focus, you draw one of the infinite potential realities that flourish all around you into mani-festation as your personal *now*. Because the Z-axis is a personal axis and you can face any direction you choose, it can also be called the axis of free will. As you point your Z-axis, you knowingly or unknowingly co-create your future.

Locating the *Now* in the Body

Imagine your own Z-axis timeline stretching infinitely in front of you and behind you with its center at the center point of your root chakra. We will engage that center point in meditation. We will often concentrate our attention on that one point exclusively. Why? Because that point is the energetic counterpart of the *now* as it exists for you. By bringing your uninterrupted awareness to that point, you access the mysteries of the infinite *now*.

Since we really only experience one point of the never-ending timeline of the Z-axis, the *now* point, meditating on this point makes a lot of sense. It brings our awareness into closer alignment with the *now*. It gathers our scattered attention from the chaos of past oriented regrets and future oriented anxiety.

We never directly experience the past or the future. We can remember the past and anticipate the future, but we always engage in these activities in the present moment, the *now*. The *now*, marked by the center point of the perineum, guides us to the link with the Infinite we seek. Since this center point of the root chakra, at the center point of the perineum, is a *point*, let's first get comfortable with the notion of a point before we get too specific about *this* particular point.

According to Euclid, a point has no parts and no dimensions. It is infinite. Every time we can imagine splitting a point in half, we simply find a smaller point. We can keep imagining the splitting of that ever-diminishing point and never get to the unsplittable point. Likewise, the center point of the root chakra is infinite.

We are accustomed to thinking of infinity as *big*, but the *point*, infinitely divisible, brings us to an infinite journey *inward*. Unlike the line of past and future (the Z-axis), which extends infinitely outward in its two polar directions, the point of *now* recedes infinitely into itself, making the *now* eternal.

At the point where your own forward pointing Z-axis passes through your root chakra, it creates within you your own *center point* along eternity. Leonardo da Vinci called this point the center point of the body because the perineum is the same distance from the top of the head as it is to the bottom of the feet. This point, where time intersects with the center of your body, I am calling *your personal now*.

Although it may seem strange to appoint an anatomical location to the more mystical notion of the *now,* you may find that by bringing your attention to the center point of the perineum, you can more easily access a true experience of the *now.* You can balance the seesaw of the distraction of past and future at the focused fulcrum of *now.* By meditating on this point, we receive many benefits. Here, disturbing past memories and fearful future projections all lose their power. We can even start to transcend concerns about death by meditating on this point.

Many people accept the notion that while the human life span is limited, the soul is eternal. Your root chakra acts as your own personal, portable portal, which connects you to your soul's immortality. The Z-axis can help you understand that you do not begin and end with the birth and death of your body. By focusing on the point of *now* in meditation, you can begin to transcend the limiting effects of your fears about death and your concerns for survival. When you understand that you have eternity to accomplish your heart's desire, what's the rush? You become more concerned with establishing a joyful rhythm than with reaching some illusory finish line.

In this simple yet mystical practice of focusing your attention on the center point of the root chakra at the perineum, something extraordinary happens. Your tiny point of *now* gives you access to all time. The center point of your very own Z-axis links you to eternity. Entering the Z-axis and its never-ending stream of *nows* helps you to create the reality you desire.

Session Two of the Practice Section assists you in aligning your Z-axis for the purpose of achieving access to the Infinite as it manifests as time.

Softening the Pain of the Past

Do painful memories haunt you and interfere with the joyful unfolding of your life? I don't know anyone who has not experienced some trauma or loss in their past. For some reason, past difficulties seem to exert a magnetic pull on the mind. Painful memories appear to involuntarily fling themselves into our awareness and dim even our bright new experiences with their grimness.

Here, it is helpful to bring our understanding of Law of Attraction into the picture. From this vantage point we see that memories do not assert themselves as autonomous malevolent forces. They are simply drawn to us through the magnetism of our previous attention to them.

Fortunately, we can transmute these memories that continue to hurt even though the event is long past. Kahlil Gibran said, "The deeper that sorrow carves into your being, the more joy you can contain."[1] One good reason for us to turn our attention to the past in meditation is to transform the role it plays in the creation of our present, and to brighten its effect on our future.

In addition to painful memories, the past frequently derails our current intentions through its masterful use of habits. Do you have habits that move you to repeat unwanted behaviors as if you were a puppet? Who doesn't? We all do it in our own unique ways. We can benefit from this tendency toward repetition by developing desirable new habits. But for now, our goal is easier. We simply want to befriend the past with all its quirks, its bumps and bruises, and its deeply carved grooves. Yes, even the ones that have us acting in ways that hurt and embarrass us. It is, after all, our own past. If we don't love it, who will?

There is one more aspect of the past worth considering before we move on. Although the past seems over, it is constantly new with the birth of every moment of *now*. Since you must turn your Z-axis all the way around to look at the past, you superimpose your past onto your future in the process. If your past was painful or undesirable in some way, the more you turn around to look at it, the more it may appear in your future as a sort of undesirable double exposure. If however, your past was satisfying, inspiring, and filled with God-awareness, then as you turn around to remember it, it provides a template for future joy and inspiration. But both the past and the future can only be perceived in the moment that they are perceived. That is, the *now*. Without the *now*, the past does not exist. Consider the possibility that the past changes with the understanding, memories, and moods you bring to it in your present awareness.

By befriending the past, we mysteriously clear the field of our future so that it becomes an opening for our most cherished dreams to come true. Through the first meditation in Session Two of the Practice Section, we shine light on the restrictive shadows that the past continually casts on the future. Then, with the future bright, clear, and open, we can move confidently into each new *now*.

This meditation begins the sacred process of discovering how you are rooted in the Infinite. In this system, we find three portals of access to the Infinite within the root chakra. Our first entrance, the Z-axis, links us through the infinity of time. Within the Z-axis we can place our attention in three different directions: backward to the past, inward to the present, or forward to the future. Each of these three directions offers a unique gaze at infinity. Because our past tends to hold our *now*, and even our future, in a grip of limitation, Session Two begins with a meditation that increases our concentration skills while we heal and release our painful past.

Welcoming the Future

Ahead of you lies all possibility. Like the past, the future also takes its existence from your personal *now*. Like a ray emanating from your *now* spotlight, your future is born anew with your present focus. As you shine the spotlight of your attention on any subject, so your future appears. Completely malleable and filled with potential, your future unfolds eternally.

When you look forward in time, you color your *now* with the filter of your anticipation. Once you have practiced the first Z-axis meditation of befriending your past, you are ready to look forward with freedom, creativity, and a full palette of colors. Look toward the potential fulfillment of every one of your dreams. See the satisfaction of all your desires. Sense the heights of experience that you seek. Looking to the future, you can enjoy all of its potential, knowing that its joyful fulfillment comes only in the *now*.

The shape of your vibration determines what you manifest as your future unfolds, but since the future never comes, what it really determines is your experience in your *now*. One good reason to turn your meditative focus to the future is to prepave your way. Abraham recommends prepaving the increments of your day for smooth and intentional creation. In the next meditation in the Practice Section, you will do a more sweeping form of this mental play.

All is *Now*

We have seen that our experience of both the past and the future takes place exclusively in the *now*. With that awareness, we can see ourselves in a globe of time where all is created in each moment: past, present, and future. We can think of the root chakra as a 3-D movie projector flashing frames at such high resolution that they create the illusion (or reality) of time behind us and in front of us. Whether you choose to call time an illusion or a reality makes no difference. We have a back and a front and whether we call it real or unreal, time exists in our consciousness.

As we close our eyes and withdraw our attention from the outside world, we lessen our awareness of front and back. As we withdraw our attention from the forward and backward limbs of the Z-axis, we bring more attention to the center point of *now*. With the third Z-axis meditation, we advance our concentration effort by circling in even closer to the center of the chakra until our attention lands on the *now* with more ease and steadiness than it did before we explored the whole Z-axis. The third Z meditation in the Practice Section focuses on the *now*.

Flowing with the Z-axis

Although the root chakra's element is earth and its major attributes are stillness and stability, this chakra's Z-axis gives us the sense of and the desire for movement forward. One of the distinguishing aspects of the human root, as compared to the plant's root, is that it can move around with us while staying firmly rooted. Because we are not rooted in the earth, we can carry the energetic essence of the earth everywhere we go. The fourth Z meditation in the Practice Section loosens your obstructions and opens your Z-axis for an easier sense of flow.

In our garden, clearing the path for the water to flow through the Z-axis promotes joyful manifestation. The Z-axis connects us with our life's journey. As we learn to align ourselves with the inner truth of the Z-axis, we develop a more harmonious relationship with others, with the material world, and with the adventure of our human incarnation. By merging your meditative awareness with your root chakra's Z-axis, you take the first important step in the alignment process. You place your vehicle squarely on the road you wish to travel.

See Session Two of the Practice Section for the experiential exercises that correspond to this chapter.

Chapter Notes

[1] Kahlil Gibran, The Prophet (New York: Alfred A. Knopf, Inc., 1923) page 29

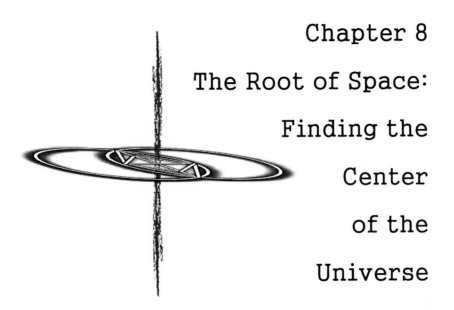

Chapter 8
The Root of Space:
Finding the
Center
of the
Universe

While time flows perpetually along the Z-axis, space stands perfectly still. All the music in the world owes its rhythm to the forward-flowing Z-axis. Every painting silently praises the motionless Y-axis.

In this chapter we heighten our spiritual awareness by befriending space. If you try to envision no-space, you will find that you cannot do it. Your sense of space is irrepressible. It keeps filling any void you attempt to imagine. Space acts as the ground of our consciousness. In the last chapter, we understood the forward flowing Z-axis to be the axis of time. Here we discover that the vertical Y-axis is the axis of space. With that discovery comes our second avenue of access to the Infinite.

As we move through this section, we find that the Y-axis of space perpetually creates our reality. It does this automatically, whether we ask it to or not. We are about to explore how that happens and how you can participate in the process so that the reality you live better matches your heart's desire.

The Y-axis also has another job. It provides spiritual upliftment, purification, and our connection with Infinite Consciousness. Although it does this automatically too, we don't necessarily perceive it unless we ask for it.

Sometimes we may bring our hands together to pray. With our fingers pointed upward, the line between our hands outlines the Y-axis. If you pray in this way, you bring yourself into alignment with the Y-axis with this simple gesture. We achieve a similar effect as we meditate with our energetic spine aligned with the vertical Y-axis. By making space in our consciousness for the Y-axis within us to breathe, divine presence can enter more easily. Spiritual awareness can more naturally replace our typically worried, angry, or pained state of mind. In other words, allowing can replace resisting as our main mode of being.

If you want to get really friendly with the Y-axis in no time at all, go into the woods and commune with the trunks of the trees. (I'm sure you've experienced this many times in your life.) Feel the resonance created as tree after tree personally expresses its urge toward the vertical. You may even feel your spine join in the chorus. Notice how your spinal column lengthens and pulls upward as it awakens to the magnetic field of the tree trunks.

As you begin opening to the presence of the Y-axis in nature, a feeling surges through your muscles as if pouring in from some infinite source. It lifts your stature like an expert hand suddenly animating a cloth puppet. As if some great burden were just released from your shoulders, you spring upward in your step, in your spirit, and in your heart. The edges of your mouth lift in a smile. You have encountered the buoyancy of the up-force.

Gravity's Secret

What up-force? The one hidden inside gravity. I don't need to introduce you to the force of gravity. You know all about it. If you ever get confused about the direction of the Y-axis, just drop something: your shoe, your pen, this book. It will instantly trace the path of the Y-axis for you, no questions asked. What it won't tell you, though, is about the up-force. In that same line of force that plunked the apple on Newton's head, there is a hidden up-force. It straightens your posture, uplifts your spirits, and heightens your perspective. It rises as reliably as the apple falls, but it doesn't do it just anywhere. Fortunately, it does do it where *you* are. This uplifting force resides in your Y-axis as it passes through your energetic spine.

The Y-axis is a two-way street. It goes down and it goes up. Just as we don't find traffic on the highway going north and south in the same lane, the Y-axis flows in two separate domains. It flows down as gravity in the outer world and up as buoyancy in the inner world.

If you have ever experienced the heaviness of fatigue or depression, it means your spirit got derailed. (And who has not experienced this?) Your inner life got caught up in the traffic of the outer realm of gravity that flows all things downward. It is because this happened to me that I have come to explore this in such detail. I am deeply grateful that I was able to receive this information through the contrast of years of extreme gravity and fatigue. It may generate even more far-reaching effects for you if you have not already changed your physical body in your escapades with misplaced gravity, as I have. Regardless of our varied physical conditions, as we enter the inner realm of the Y-axis, we can all catch a ride on the elevator of pure spirit.

Finding Here

If you take a piece of string and lay it out straight on your kitchen table, you'll have a mini Z-axis. That's your timeline. Now, if you take your finger from above and point down to the center of the string, your finger becomes the Y-axis. From the perspective of the string (the Z-axis of time), your finger touches the center point of time, which is *now*. From the point of view of your finger (the

Y-axis of space), the string touches the center point of space, which is *here*. One point, two names. Just as you may walk into a doorway and call it an entrance, and walk out the same doorway and call it an exit, when we approach the *now* from the angle of the vertical Y-axis, we will call it by a different name. We will call it *here*. We may even feel inclined to give it a few more names as it reveals its many functions.

We don't hear much about *here*. *Now* gets all the attention. That's because the *here* is not such a mystical concept. After all, we know we are here. Even in our regular day-to-day consciousness, totally identified with the body, we deduce that we are *here*, but there is more.

In the same way that the point of *now* is eternal, infinite, and gives us access to all time, the point of *here* is infinitely vast and gives us access to all space. The center point of the root chakra, this point of *now* and *here*, is more than just the center of your body. It is also the center of your consciousness.

What a strange place to find the center of consciousness. It seems like some sort of mistake. But just as the door provided an entrance or exit depending on the angle and context of our view, the root chakra provides many functions within our consciousness. The function we perceive depends on the angle from which we perceive it. As we look through the lens of the Y-axis, among the many functions of the root chakra, we find the unquestionable role of the center point of consciousness.

In 1971, Ram Dass wrote the book *Be Here Now*[1] and altered the path of a generation. Like a kaleidoscopic unfolding of color, minds were opening to new dimensions of experience and *Be Here Now* aptly became the password for that journey. In the Yoga of Alignment, we find that the meeting point of the vertical Y-axis and the forward flowing Z-axis at the center of the root chakra energetically utters, "here-now." As we enter this point from the doorway of the Y-axis, we access another aspect of its mystical potential. We are in the process of uncovering tangible entrance to the continuous *here-now* at the core of our being, and doing this, our garden bursts with color.

Introducing the Egg

You may live in Los Angeles or Paris. You may be sprawled out under an oak tree or squeezed into a rush hour bus. It makes no difference if you are soaking in the bubble bath of luxury or bent under unbearable burdens. No matter where you are, I know you have your root chakra with you. Right at the point where your Y-axis passes through your root chakra, that is where you are. Why that point? Because that is the point of *here*.

Let's look at the meditator in the illustration. His Y-axis dominates the picture. The Y-axis is his core just as it is yours and mine. We are calling the part of the Y-axis that fits in your physical body your energetic spine. Whereas the Z-axis passed quickly through the body, hardly taking up any more space than the length of the chakra itself, the Y-axis lingers. It runs through your entire spine, and your full-standing frame aligns with its vertical intention. It pierces all seven chakras and links them into a united system like pearls on a string.

The Z-axis had anatomical landmarks to define its boundaries, but the Y-axis of the root chakra has no such flags. The vertical axis passes through the perineum claiming a portion of the space above (inside the body) and a portion of the space below (outside the body) the center point of the chakra.

This small vertical segment of the Y-axis passes vertically through the *here-now* point of the root chakra. It has an energy field around it shaped like an elongated egg. This egg sits half inside, half outside the body. This egg defines the shape and location of the vertical dimension of the chakra.

What does this mean? When an axis passes through a body, the abstract marries the concrete. Meaning is born. In the case of the Z-axis, past and future are established. Life and death are named. You call the story your life.

The abstract Y-axis similarly mingles with the body to make meaning, but it doesn't take its cues from our anatomy like the more personal Z-axis did. Instead, it becomes a link between the inner and outer worlds and, at its very center, it is the center of all space.

When we looked at the Z-axis, it was easy to believe that the center point of *now* was the center of time. After all, the *now* seems evenly placed between the eternities of past and future. But when I suggest that the center point of *here* is the center point of space, it might bring up some resistance. It feels too literal and seems to imply that your perineum is the center of everyone's universe, and that seems too egotistical, too naïve, and just too weird.

Weird but workable. The vertical egg at the center of your body acts as a link. This link bolts you to the center of the universe. That is its job. It defines *here*. Together we will see how the egg at your root chakra is the center of the universe. I think you'll find that it gives us a very useful way of looking at how we are connected to the universe in which we live.

The Center of the Universe is Still

If this egg is the center of the universe, what are you doing sitting on it? We tend to think of the center of the universe as a singular, distant, unmapped location in outer space, but we are gong to trade in that understanding for one that ultimately will make more sense. Let's consider the possibility that the center of the universe is in you and in me and in everyone else, too. This is not really news. The seventeenth century mathematician and philosopher Blaise Pascal stated it most eloquently when he said, "Nature is an infinite sphere whose center is everywhere and circumference nowhere."

We each have direct personal access to many centers of the universe. We will focus on the one at the root chakra. You have a *here-now* egg silently birthing your reality through your unique center of the universe. Can you feel the power of that?

Through meditation you can experience this egg. Once you find it, you begin to know unquestionably that you are bolted to the center of the universe. You will know you have found it first by sensing in meditation its egg-shaped presence half inside you and half below you at the location of the root chakra. But more importantly, it reveals its true identity with an extraordinary, transformational stillness. This stillness defies description.

Since the egg's stillness exists in the inner realm and does not take well to words, it might help to look to an outer model for elaboration. Just like the pictures in an anatomy book help us imagine what our organs look like even though we can't see them, a well-established tree can help us know what our root feels like even if we cannot yet sense it.

The next time you are outside, find a tree you like. Push it. Try to move it. Try to pull it out of the ground. (Don't worry, you will only tickle the tree.) Can you feel the unshakable stillness of its roots? In the tree you encounter enormous stability. Plants are our gurus on the subject of roots, but as we already know, their roots keep them bolted to the earth, immobile. You and I have a different kind of root. The egg is our root. It takes a different form because it has a different function. Our root, with strength and stability like the tree's root, bolts us not to the earth, but to the center of the universe. This is how the Y-axis keeps us rooted in the Infinite.

The tree's root is still because it is rooted in the stillness of the earth. Our root is still because it is rooted in the earth element, but there is a more far-reaching source of this stillness. The egg, our root, is the center of the universe and it is the only point in the universe that *is* still. Everything else moves. The center is absolute stillness.

Twin Realities

As if all this weren't enough, there is still more to be revealed at this root point of *here-now*. It is not only the center of consciousness and the center of the universe. The first chakra also unmasks the mystery of what is *self* and what is *other*. As we progress through the Y-axis you may feel inclined to trade in your habitual understanding of who you are for a broader, more transcendent identity. Making practical use of the Y-axis' link to the Infinite allows the flow of joy and the release of many burdens.

Who are you? If you are like most of us, you tend to think of yourself as ending at your skin. It's pretty logical. Body logic is based on input from the senses and action of the muscles. You have sensation only up to edge of your skin. Beyond that, you have no feeling, so you unconsciously (or consciously) conclude that anything outside your skin must not be you. That makes sense. It works the same way with your muscles. You can move your own arm with your thought, but you can't move your friend's arm with your thought. Therefore, your arm must be you, and his arm must be him. The logic is, if you can't move it, it's not yours.

I don't want to underestimate this very useful sense of body-as-self and other-as-not-self. It allows us to function in the world and with each other in a way that makes relationship possible. I use it every time I say "I" or "you." You use it when you cash your pay-check, hug your children, and put on your socks. It serves us in all the day-to-day functions we depend on. We'd be lost without it.

Let's go back to our friend in the illustration and let's clearly mark the inside of his body as *self* and the outside of his body as *other*. This picture describes the relationship between the body and con-sciousness from the perspective of the small self or ego. We spend most of our life act-ing from this point of view. It works for us on countless practical levels, but many wise souls have noticed that it also causes much pain when it urges us to perceive ourselves as separate, disconnected beings.

other

self

Let's not throw the small self away in our attempt to advance spiri-tually. Let's embrace it as we would a child, and notice that, as we com-passionately regard this identity, we ourselves must be *other* than it. Who, then, is the embracer? Who offers this compassion to the one we thought we were just a minute ago?

We switched angles. Suddenly we are looking through the eyes of the higher Self or Inner Being. Where is it in our illustration? From our new vantage point, outside the body corresponds to the higher Self or Atman, which is *other* than the ego (which stays *within* the body.)

Is the door an exit or an entrance? Both. Is the center point *here* or is it *now*? Both. Is my perception of myself my true Self, or is it simply ego? Both. Is that which I perceive as the universe other than me, or is it my higher Self? Both. Different names based on differ-ent perspectives. Different functions based on different needs.

When you need to tie your shoelace, the body is your self. It does the job masterfully. We praise it. When you seek unconditional love and the body-based identity activates conflicting concerns, we condemn it. When you walk to the bookstore to buy a book on how to experience unconditional love, your small self carries your body there in excellent fashion. Bravo! When you sit to meditate as instructed in your new book, your body-based identity chats on and on about tying shoelaces and walking to bookstores. It's a big problem. You scold it. Different moments, different perspectives, different values.

In this system, we look to honor our divinity and have compassion for our humanity. The more we can recognize ourselves as extraordinary mixtures of human and divine essence, the richer our experience becomes. As we look at others, we learn to hold the same vision. Honoring our divinity and having compassion for our humanity, we experience our wholeness more easily than by trying to eliminate ego.

In fact, the ego usually tries to eliminate itself thinking it will get great spiritual acclaim from that accomplishment, but of course it doesn't really want to eliminate itself. (We will revisit this idea in Chapter 12.) So it keeps chasing its own tail and spinning you around until you're dizzy. But then again, when your dog chases his tail, you think it's cute and funny, and you get out the video camera. See if you can adore your ego in the same, non-identified way.

Transcendent Self

ego

Back to the illustration. We previously labeled it according to the perspective of the small self where inside the skin is *self* and outside the skin is *other*. But now we have new meanings for inner and outer. Let's add the labels that apply when we are identified with the higher Self where inside the skin is the body-identified ego, and outside (plus inside) the skin is the transcendent Self or Atman.

The Mystical Link

Builders used to use small wooden pegs to join together two pieces of wood. Those pegs, sitting half in one piece and half in the other, would bind those two pieces of wood together to function as one. The egg performs the same function at the root chakra. It holds two things together. With all the stability of the earth element, it acts as a bond.

What two things does it link together? That depends on how you answer the question, "Who am I?" How you identify yourself might not seem to be of great consequence to a chakra, but it determines which function of the link becomes active.

Remember mood rings? They would change color if you were angry or happy or sad. Well, at least that's what they were supposed to do. Whether you still have your favorite mood ring stashed away somewhere or you thought they were a bunch of hooey right from the start doesn't really matter here. You can still imagine that this link acts like a mystical mood ring. As you identify with your small self or ego, your link functions differently from when you shift your identity into the transcendent Self, or Atman. Like a mood ring changing colors, your link transforms its function depending on whom you choose to be. How does this work?

Let's start with our ordinary, day-to-day state of consciousness. When the ego state is active, the egg bolts you to the center of the universe. It acts as a link that connects self and other. When you bring awareness to the egg, even from your ego state, it benefits you. It harmonizes the outside world making it friendly to you. It smooths your business dealings, keeps traffic flowing, and improves communication in your relationships. It makes living as an "in"dividual in an "outer" world of others a gratifying experience.

Since we all know that living the life of an ego on earth can be painful, embarrassing, frustrating, enraging, etc., accessing this link can make life more livable and enjoyable for the weary ego.

What is the egg's function from the point of view of the transcendent Self? When we are identified in a way that does not end at the skin, the link joins two aspects of the Self. From here, the egg bolts you to the center of the Self. The inner half sits within the individual ego body. The outer half of the link extends into the great, undifferentiated infinite aspect of each of us, which is pure being. Now, identified with the "outer" Universal Self, the link harmonizes the "inner" ego realm with the higher Self. It makes your unique instrument (body, mind, personality) the focal point of the great artwork that is your life.

If you are functioning through the faculties of your higher Self, which you may be doing more and more these days, then the link becomes a bridge that keeps your personality in alignment with your heart's desire and your soul's intention. It provides access to union with the Infinite, with God. This is the goal of yoga. This linking function is essential to our work. To amplify its activity in your life, turn to the Y-axis exercises in the Practice Section. By bringing your consciousness into resonance with this sacred link through meditation, you increase your access to all its blessings.

See Session Three of the Practice Section for the experiential exercises that correspond to this chapter.

Chapter Notes

---

[1] Ram Dass, *Be Here Now* (San Cristobal, New Mexico: Lama Foundation, 1971)

Chapter 9
Transformation and Creation: Cosmic Potential

et's talk about how the ego can lead to enlightenment. Actually, I am using the word "enlightenment" without a license. Not living in that transcendent state, I still dare to use the word, but with a modified meaning—one we can all put our arms around. When I speak of "enlightenment" here, I am referring to the *bringing in of light*, the *allowing of light* within the dense, dark clutter of a more resistant state of consciousness. Maybe a better word would be "enbrightenment."

This light comes from within, but you may wonder, from within what? We now have two different meanings for inner and outer. When you are identified with the small self, *inner* means yourself while *outer* means other. It is usually from this perspective (of ego) that we sit down to meditate. As we focus on the center point of the root chakra and its Y-axis, even in this state, the egg may become perceptible.

Because we are identified with the small self, the egg is in the mode of linking self and other. It bridges the gap between our individual consciousness and the world in which we live. It transforms the world from hostile to friendly.

Once your consciousness enters the egg/link, you experience the connection, and eventually the oneness, between self and other. This is a pivotal moment. With this realization, the mood ring starts to change colors.

Within the egg, the ego steps into rhythm with the transcendent Self. That which was perceived as *other* just a minute ago begins to transform. *Other* begins to reveal itself as pure consciousness. What the ego understood as *other*, the higher Self understands as part of *Self*. With this realization, the link shifts into its higher function. We find ourselves no longer at the center of the link between self and other. We are now at the center of the link between self and Self. What we thought of as the center of the universe reveals itself as the center of the Self. The link is suddenly connecting ego with Atman. We walk through.

Since the link has this dual function, even if you enter it from ego, you can leap levels. Like getting a fashion makeover, you can enter with your scraggly old ego, and exit as your luminous transcendent Self. The egg transmutes your point of view. It is *here*. It is also *now*. It links self and other. It also links self and Self. The link works perpetually on all levels. It is up to us to cross the bridge.

You Are Everywhere

In meditation, when you experience yourself as bolted to the center of the universe, there is a tremendous shift in consciousness. You will understand yourself to be continuous with the universe via the adapter of the link. With that awareness, it becomes obvious that the vehicle of your body is not separate from the Universal whole. Your individual identity is like a wave in the ocean. It is a highly organized and recognizable pattern of energy with which you have become identified. But now, through this link, you connect with that eternal, all expansive Atman or true Self.

What you once thought of as the "outer" universe, the domain of astronomers and physicists, now reveals itself to you as your own being. We saw that from the perspective of the higher Self, the link bolts you to the center of the Self. The truth experienced at the center of the Z-axis, the *now* point along the infinity of time, turned out to be all time, eternal. Now, we see that right at the center point of the Y-axis, at the *here* point within the infinity of space, we are *everywhere*. How does this happen?

The transcendent Self has no limits. Once you shift your identity from the body-identified self to the all-inclusive Self, you find that you are not only *here*, but you are *everywhere*. You discover that the infinite expanse of space that you previously considered "*other*," or "*out there*," is none other than the 3-D projection of cosmic consciousness through the focusing power of your individual perspective. When your individual ego consciousness chooses to focus on the root chakra link, you can find your oneness with the entire universe. Once that connection becomes real, ego transforms and aligns with Atman, and the center of the universe becomes the center of the Self. It is not your ego that is everywhere. It is your true Self.

Now we have touched our second infinity. The well kept secret of the vastness of space that exists in the infinitely small point of *here*, is now yours.

The Big Bang of Your Reality

The Y-axis has no contact with the flow of time. It shares only one point with the Z-axis of time, the point of *now*. That is why space is so still. It knows only *now*. We used the tree's root to help us imagine the utter stillness of our own root. The tree's stability offers only a hint of the stability that lives inside you waiting to be tapped. But what good is stillness?

From this absolute stillness comes all activity or what we call creation. Unwittingly, we funnel our personal perspective into manifestation through the focusing power of the egg. This odd-shaped egg embodies the universal creative principle. Georg Feuerstein describes its influence (as it is acknowledged in yoga as the lingam) as, "the unimaginable potency or power of creativity prior to creation of the world."[1]

By straddling the inner and outer worlds, the egg occupies both the location and moment of creation (*here* and *now*). The space on your Y-axis below the root chakra is non-physical. It has not yet stepped into specific form. It holds all potential creation in its primordial expanse. But once it crosses that threshold into the body, once it takes on form, it begins its developmental journey toward becoming a distinct moment of *now*. The instant that happens, your reality is born. That event corresponds to the "big bang" that scientists talk about when referring to the creation of the universe. But from the point of view of consciousness, that was not a singular event. It occurs at the birthplace of every single moment of *now*. That birthplace is *here*.

Does that mean that the entire universe is created over and over again for each quickly forgotten, hardly-perceptible moment of now? Perpetually. Your human egg-shaped root links you with the cosmic stillness prior to creation while continually exploding into form.

The stillness that lives in you here at the boundary between your individuality and the vast, undifferentiated universe acts as your own personal font of creative life force. The egg of the Y-axis stands half in the great oneness before all distinctions, and half within the specific boundaries that bear your name. "I" begins here.

Being Born Now

Remember the Z-axis? The axis of time places the future in front of us and the past behind us. But the Y-axis knows nothing about forward and backward. It speaks only the language of above and below. At the point where it crosses the Z-axis, it gets to experience the *now*. That is its entire encounter with time: *now*. It cannot even conceive of past or future. It does not live in that dimension.

At that center point of *here*, the forward flowing Z-axis also gets its only taste of space. And since time gets only that one point of space, it cannot conceive of *there*. When it comes to space, time only knows *here*. You can start to see why the intersection of these two axes, the dynamic point of *here* and *now*, merits so much of our attention. Especially when it lands right in the center of your body.

What all this means to your Y-based egg is that it can only do its huge job of cosmic creation in one infinitely receding point, one eternally evolving point called the *here-now*. If the "big bang" of the creation of the universe is perpetual, that means you too are perpetually being born. You were not born long ago and then the birthing stopped. Your personal creation is as ongoing as the *now*. The past has no meaning to its creative intention. Your birth emerges continuously from the formless stillness in every moment of *now*.

With this understanding, we can take a completely different approach to all of our so-called problems. No matter how entrenched they may seem, we can totally reinterpret illness, poverty, depression, and loss. We can see that every infinitely small interval of *now* offers a potential pivot. We are in possession of a never-ending stream of creation that can change direction at any and every moment. As bleak as things might seem, a new big bang, with all its cosmic potential, is as close as your next *now*.

I know this is hard to believe. It may sound fine intellectually, but what if you are dealing with a chronic illness or a lifetime of addiction? If you are facing prejudice or the devastation of war, how can this possibly be of any practical use? Can your egg really fix all these problems?

I would only be able to answer this question with authority if I myself had full mastery of this system. And since that is far from the case, I can merely offer this simple question in return: What have you got to lose? All any of us has to lose are our problems. By opening, little by little, to the font of creation within us, we naturally shed our victim skin. In this process in which light comes in to replace dense, old belief systems, new life springs into view. Your spirit illuminates the young green leaves of spring.

Given the chance, new creation will convince you of its genuineness. The principle I am describing will manifest itself so beautifully in your life that you will cry tears of joy. All we need is a way to begin to open to the possibility of ongoing creation. We need a practical method for weaving this nice little theory of infinite potential into the nitty-gritty of our experience. Otherwise it is just a mental exercise with little to offer us. But if we can feel the actual power of the creative activity just behind the veil of form, if we can sense its readiness to create something different from what it molded in the last moment, then we are making space for the light to shine in.

One way to accomplish all this is through meditation. Meditation on the Y-axis of the root chakra promotes clarity. It quiets the mind and cultivates inner peace. By finding inner peace, we gain access to different options for creating our reality. We are no longer stuck in the time-defined cycle of re-creating the past in the future. When we enter the center point of *here-now*, we regain a full palette of colors. Our creative spirit is free to express itself in whatever way we choose.

Entering the egg in meditation offers such an all-pervasive sense of peace that it can erase your usual perceptual reality. Although this experience can transform us in wonderful ways, we probably don't want to remain there forever. What kind of life would that be, always still, always close to the undifferentiated oneness?

Universal Intelligence has solved that problem in the true spirit of entertainment. There are Y-axes and Z-axes intersecting everywhere, but when a human root chakra inhabits one of those crossroads, that point becomes a front row seat on the miracle ride of life. The mystical meeting of these two dimensions manufactures an illusion of cosmic proportion.

Cosmic Cartoons

We have more in common with Bugs Bunny than you might think. The universe gives us the illusion of movement much like we give cartoons to our children. In just about any cartoon you will find the main character in something called a walk cycle. The character is drawn in eight or so different phases of walking. With legs and arms in different positions, each drawing of Bugs or Daffy or Mickey or SpongeBob occupies the same location on its own individual, transparent cel. The background is then moved behind the character, frame by frame, in the opposite direction of the way the character is going. If the background moves to the left, it gives the illusion that Bugs is heading right. But if you drop out the background, even a small child will see that Bugs is bolted to the center of the screen.

Similarly, the universe is moving our background and we are buying it. We accept it as reality. And joyfully so. It is as delightful a gift as are cartoons to a child. The movement of time through the Z-axis gives us the illusion of movement through space. But just as Bugs Bunny is bolted to the center of the screen, we are bolted to the center of the universe. When we bring our attention to the Y-axis with uninterrupted concentration, we reduce our perception of the Z-axis, and therefore of time. The background stops moving. We realize that space is like a 3-D movie screen that has been displaying time's elaborate moving background. Once it is revealed, we realize that we are always *here*. And *here* never moves.

As virtual reality technology becomes more sophisticated and more common, it will provide an even more compelling outer world model for this phenomenon. It will become more believable that each of us contains a still center around which the universe performs. And don't forget, *everyone* is the center of the universe. It is indeed a very generous and abundant universe.

Cartoons may be one thing, but what about the "real world"? If the center of the universe is in your root chakra, does the sun revolve around you? We see the sun low on the horizon, then high in the sky, and then back down again on the other side of the horizon. Left to our naked senses, the earth stands still and the heavenly bodies move around us. We don't feel the earth moving. In fact, sitting in your parked car, we would measure your speed as zero. However, should we change the perspective of our measurements, we would find you are hurtling through space at over 100 miles per second.

Yes, in spite of what we see and feel every day of our lives, we have come to believe the word of the scientists. We are convinced that the concepts of "sunrise" and "sunset," beautiful and poetic though they may be, are misnomers. It is definitely the Earth that is moving.

But if your perineum is bolted to the motionless center of the universe, how can you move? The tree, our rooted teacher, can't walk. We can. What's the difference? How can your center of the universe be perfectly still and yet move with you when you ride the bus, drive your car, or as you simply stand on this constantly moving earth? Can the formless stillness move?

Slowing Down Time

We have a big dilemma. Is your center of the universe still or does it move with you? From the perspective of the root chakra, no matter how much you appear to move, your center remains stable and absolutely still. Everything else moves around it. That means that if you appear to walk forward, you are really staying in the same place and the universe is moving toward you. The whole world becomes a big treadmill from this perspective. There is absolute, immovable stability at the egg. This statement may seem outrageous, but it helps to remember that these realities live in a realm apart from our usual waking state of consciousness. This statement describes reality from the perspective of one isolated axis, the Y-axis.

In our culture, ruled largely by the outer directed, Z-axis-oriented sciences, "objective reality" is highly valued. This works out very well for us as we use our cell phones, surf the Internet, and drive our automobiles. We experience the miraculous advances in science and technology in just about every area of our lives on a daily basis. In the inner directed sciences, however, more value is placed on "experiential reality."

Without judging one reality more important or valid than the other, we focus here on the latter. In the spirit of respect for the co-existence of both realities, we can say that as the earth sails through space, it carries six billion, absolutely still, human clad centers of the universe with it.

But to talk about the earth's movement, or any movement for that matter, we must include time. Without time, our experience becomes a still snapshot. We need many images projected over time, like the frames of a movie, in order to experience movement. Movement can only happen in time. It requires time to move from here to there.

So to find the place where we touch the undifferentiated, pre-creation stillness, it helps to remove, or lessen, the presence of time. We can do that by staying keenly focused on the vertical axis which has minimal access to time. With our faculties focused exclusively on the Y-axis, we reduce our awareness of time.

Letting go of the habitual Z-axis awareness in meditation removes us temporarily from some of the forces of time. Remember that the Y-axis still includes the center point of all axes. Therefore, it includes the point of *now* without the clutter of past and future. Even this small shift in our usual participation with time greatly diminishes our perception of movement. The curtain opens and we behold a level of stillness we have never before imagined. It doesn't matter if this perception is brief or enduring since it is an out-of-time experience. It touches us and we are never the same.

Stepping out of the realm of time (by staying focused on the Y-axis) slows down the passage of time. If you concentrate your mind on the Y-axis component of the root chakra, you will find you have more time in the day to get things done. You may find yourself looking at your watch in amazement. This practice holds you in the *now* and also creates inner stillness (not to be confused with outer stillness).

Sitting Still

Outer stillness (keeping your body still) has another effect. It takes us to the realm of space and holds us in the mystical *here*. To get a better sense of this, let's see how movement helps us know where we are in space. Just as we have light sensitive cells in the retina of the eye, or touch sensitive cells in the skin, we also have specialized nerve cells that tell us about our position in space. How far one hand is from the other, where an itch is and how to get your hand there to scratch it, these are the jobs of the proprioceptive cells. The majority of these receptors reside in joints, and rather than being stimulated by light or touch like the eyes or skin, they are awakened by movement.

Therefore, when we sit still in meditation, we quiet the mechanism that tells us about our physical body's spatial relationships. This serves as a good argument for controlling the fidgeting during meditation. The more quiet this physical sense is, the more receptive we can be to other dimensions of space within our consciousness.

Chapter Notes

[1] Georg Feuerstein, The Shambhala Encyclopedia of Yoga (Boston, Massachusetts: Shambhala, 1997) page 169

Meditation
awakens our awareness of
inner space in a way that cannot
be achieved by reading about it. When
we were talking about the Z-axis and its
relation to time, we focused on the center
point of *now*. We found the *now* to be infinite
and, therefore, eternal. Meditation will reveal the
same about the center point of space. The Y-axis of
the root chakra, the axis of space, renames the point
we have been calling *now* and calls it *here*. We find this
point to be the center of consciousness as well as the
center of the universe. We also find it to be the meeting
place of self and other. The Y-axis component of the
root chakra can be experienced as an elongated egg-
shaped energetic structure sitting half inside and half
outside the body. The egg acts as a link joining self
and other. It also links ego and Atman. Through
meditation, it allows us to encounter the vitalizing up-force resident within the energetic
spine. Its transformational presence
brings light into the density of ego
and flows life force into the
garden.

Chapter 10

The Root of

Being:

Balance and

Healing

Have you seen the redwood trees in northern California? Did you know that these awe-inspiring trees, which can reach heights of over 300 feet and can live for thousands of years, have relatively shallow roots? Why don't they just tip over? They support their extraordinary height with an underground network of *horizontal* roots that can extend outward for hundreds of feet.

The little tomato plants in my garden would also benefit from more horizontal roots. To stimulate this growth, when I place my young plants in the ground, I bury their bottom most leaves. Those leaves wither underground to be replaced by a strong network of horizontal roots that support and nourish my plants. They won't grow into redwoods, but they will produce many more tomatoes.

Even though our human root is invisible and nonphysical, like the redwood, it has a horizontal component that can contribute to our health and longevity. And like the little tomato plants, when we strengthen that component we become more robust and more productive. Increased health and stamina promise to reward our journey into the horizontal X-axis of the root chakra. Let's begin exploring this third dimension of access to the Infinite offered to us by our uniquely human root.

As a student of anatomy, I had always heard the perineum (the anatomical location of the root chakra) defined as the space between the genitals (front boundary) and the anus (back boundary). In my mind, this suggested a linear space along the front-to-back Z-axis of the body. As a student of yoga I had also read about the first chakra in the same location, also suggestive of the Z-axis.

But the energy of the perineum does not just move forward and backward as its anatomical description might suggest. And it doesn't just go up and down like the plant's root that we tend to use in visualization. It also goes left and right. This powerful flow of life force that moves side to side through the perineum performs an essential job in maintaining our well-being. The X-axis of the root chakra, rarely if ever acknowledged or explored, hums with powerful healing activity. This unsung hero has much to teach us about how we can augment our own healing.

As Above So Below, Brains and All

It may seem strange, but the side-to-side dimension of the bottom of your torso lives to serve you. Its purpose in your energetic anatomy is to balance and heal you. It offers the mundane facade of mild-mannered X-axis of the perineum, but it constantly works its superpowers on your behalf. In order to fully grasp how this healing dimension of the root chakra functions, it will help to relax our rigid notions of reality. An inter-dimensional activity occurs at this chakra and we want to maximize its potential.

The energy of the root chakra that moves sideways through the perineum does its job in a most unusual way. It oversees the healing process in much the same way that Clark Kent protected the people of Metropolis. We all knew that Clark and Superman were the same guy, but to the unsuspecting people of Metropolis, this was a *big* secret. Like Clark Kent, the X-axis of the perineum also hides its true energetic identity. Well it did, until now.

The startling energetic truth about the X-axis of the perineum is that it has a mystical relationship with the X-axis clothed in the corpus callosum of the brain. The corpus callosum is the name for a thick band of X-axis fibers that connects the two cerebral hemispheres allowing communication between the left and right sides of the brain. Although physically the perineum and the corpus callosum may be two different structures, and although one seems lowly and useless while the other seems wise and powerful, these two structures are *energetically* identical. They are not *like* each other, or *analogues* of each other. They are energetically the *same*. Clark Kent's grey suit and glasses were disguise enough to throw everybody off the track. Same thing here. But let all of Metropolis know, from an energetic standpoint, the perineum *is* the corpus callosum.

What does that mean? It means that when you invite Clark over for dinner, Superman gets fed. It means that what you do to one, you do to both. When you focus your attention on the root chakra, you bring awareness to the higher energy centers. When you encourage the flow of life force through the perineum, you increase energetic communication within the brain. And there is more.

On an energetic level, the buttocks echo the cerebral hemispheres. That means that when you circulate energy through the root chakra and include the buttocks in the loop, you stimulate energy movement in the brain. An energetically balanced and vitalized brain promotes healing.

Here's another way of looking at this. If we were in a room with two pianos and I played middle C on one piano, then you played middle C on the other, we would hear the sameness of the two notes. It would not seem strange that the same note could reside in two different locations. But when I tell you that the energetic presence of the perineum and the energetic presence of the corpus callosum are the same, it may not seem so obvious.

Walking Wormholes

I hope the physicists reading this section will forgive me as I attempt to convince you that your spine is a wormhole. In the Yoga of Alignment, we have been using the X, Y, and Z-axes to map out both the body and consciousness. This system fits like an old pair of jeans. It's comfortable, familiar, and reliable. That's because it is based on the view of reality to which we are so accustomed, the one touted by classical physics. It not only matches our experience, it matches our mental tendencies. We like to think that space is separate from time. We enjoy looking at the night sky and imagining it going on and on forever in what we think of as the straight line of our vision. It all makes perfect sense to us. We are even comfortable with the mysteries.

The reason we have been using the language of classical physics up to this point is simple. We use it for the same reason we use classical physics to calculate the speed of a car or to decide to bend our knees when lifting a box of books. The laws of classical physics apply in these cases and so we use them. But scientists have found that the further out into space they set their focus, the less the old rules apply. Studying distances and speeds far beyond our earthbound driving and lifting, scientists have drawn many conclusions that can easily seem illogical and counter-intuitive to us. Here on earth, as we concern ourselves with gas mileage and the prevention of low back pain, these discoveries, while mind boggling, at times seem irrelevant.

On the mystical path, we embark on a first-hand study of inner space. It has begun to occur to many people that inner space is not so different from outer space. Suddenly the vast distances and time-altering speeds of outer space seem less strange and more applicable to our lives. There may even be something here that can help accelerate our healing.

If this is so, then we have a rich opportunity for healing and spiritual upliftment within the root chakra as we borrow the notion of wormholes from the physicists and apply it to the energetic spine. If we can develop confidence in the sameness of the energetic perineum and the energetic corpus callosum, if we can trust that the X-axis of the root chakra and the X-axis of the higher chakras are identical, then we will be well on our way to experiencing wholeness. Let's see if the concept of the wormhole can take us there.

The hardest part of talking about wormholes is that they don't exist in three-dimensional space like we do. If they exist at all, they are thought to live in what scientists call hyperspace. That basically means that they have more dimensions to move around in than we do in our logical XYZ matrix. Since wormholes can function in dimensions to which we do not have access, their behavior seems bizarre and their existence seems doubtful to our everyday minds. But physicists tell us that wormholes are mathematically much more likely to exist than we would think.

So what is a wormhole? It is a short tunnel that connects two unimaginably distant locations. Let's see how we can apply this idea.

Imagine walking out of your New York bedroom, going down the hall past the bathroom, and opening the door to Paris. That does not even begin to convey the magnitude of decrease in distance rendered by wormholes. In these mysterious passageways, tens of light-years (one light-year is 5.88 trillion miles) between galaxies can be traveled over the distance of about a half-mile. These shortcuts rely on hyperspace, a medium outside our three dimensions, to do their magic. If we have access to something similar to hyperspace within our consciousness, then we might encounter unimaginable, illogical inner realities that would be very difficult to explain. If one of these were located between the top and bottom of the energetic spine, it might produce the effect we are pondering.

If the spine houses a wormhole, then the measurable three or so feet between the perineum and the corpus callosum would be analogous to the long route between galaxies. But the wormhole of the spine, accessible through meditation, reduces those three feet so drastically, that there is no perceptible space between them. We experience the perineum and the corpus callosum as occupying the same space at the same time. In other words, for all intents and purposes, they are the same thing.

As we walk around in our conscious reality, we carry this wormhole everywhere, unknowingly. It is silent. It is vast. It is extraordinary. But we are so unaware of it that my long explanation may not have swayed you at all. How can a wormhole exist inside of you? Wouldn't you know it if an inter-dimensional reality were constantly present within your body? Maybe not. Are you aware of your spleen? How about your aorta? They are quietly tucked in their places, drawing no attention to themselves, doing their job to further your life experience. Why not add a wormhole to the list of imperceptibly functioning organs? Of course the wormhole would go on the list of energetic structures, along with the chakras.

This wormhole would effectively eliminate the inner length of the Y-axis of the spine. With no inner distance from the bottom of the energetic spine to the top, we would experience the sameness of the two X-axis structures, which, from the outside, we label as the root chakra and the crown chakra. With this new understanding of the inter-dimensional sameness of above and below within the body, we can call upon the X-axis to serve us more directly. Where before you might not have thought about using root chakra X-axis meditations to improve brain functioning and overall healing, now you might.

The wormhole in the energetic spine acts as a mystical passageway within the physical spine, and it performs its inter-dimensional function whether we are aware of it or not. We are walking wormholes. The transverse energy band in the perineum resonates with the transverse band in the brain and together these two set up our field of being. If the two pianos are in tune, they sound beautiful. If we are in tune, we feel great. Let's begin moving energy through the X-axis of the root chakra and creating a sympathetic flow in the brain. Let's invite Clark Kent over for dinner so Superman gets fed.

Infinity Contained

The infinity we can access through the X-axis behaves a little differently from the other two infinities we've already considered. We visualized the Z-axis extending infinitely forward and backward (Chapter 7), and the Y-axis extending infinitely upward and downward (Chapter 8) from the root chakra. They rooted us in the infinities of time and space, respectively. They placed us in the universe. The X-axis does not root us in an infinity of universal proportion. It stays inside our system to reveal the infinity within. As the axis of *being*, it flows mostly within the space of the physical body, giving us a sense of who we are. By circulating within the buttocks, it stays close to the center point of the root chakra, continually awakening the point of *here* along the Y-axis (Chapter 8) and the point of *now* along the Z axis (Chapter 7). *Who* is here now? *You* are! That is the X-axis contribution.

The X-axis is personal. It curves back into itself creating the infinity symbol or lemniscate. In fact, the letter X can be found at the center of that symbol. The constant flow of energy along the circulating X-axis perpetually taps the center point of the chakra. It keeps that center point of *here-now* personal by perpetually placing *you* there. It puts the *be* in the formula *be-here-now*.

See Session Four of the Practice Section for the experiential exercises that correspond to this chapter.

Chapter 11
The Open
Moment

W hen you hold a prism to the light you can watch all color break free from the invisible realm. In the silence hides all sound. The freshly seeded earth secretly harbors the season's harvest. Our personal moment of *here-now* is similarly encoded with all the love, joy, wisdom, health, success, and divine revelation we could ever desire. This moment is no more than an opening, a light. We are its prism. What is coming through right now?

Aligning your root, as you have been doing (or are about to do when you explore the Practice Section), sets the stage for the outpouring of your inspired reality. Every moment offers a new opportunity for creation. As your life emerges through the opening of the *now*, you continually participate, consciously or unconsciously, in the creation of your experience. That's why we have been taking the time to develop expertise in the anatomy and physiology of the root chakra. Studying the nature of your link to the Infinite and experiencing that connection establishes sturdy roots in your garden. The life of spirit grows bountifully from such efforts.

So far, we have been exploring the three dimensions in which we live and discovering how each individually contributes to our root. Now it is time to put it all together. You are growing intimate with the many functions of the root chakra. As we reassemble and synthesize, you may find that something feels different. Awakening may replace some areas of unconsciousness. Disinterest fades as inspiration grows. The open moment of *here-now* captures your attention. How could this ever have been boring? It is all there is.

The gift of the root chakra has become clear. It births each *now*. To review, here is the recipe:

- The Z-axis provides the *now*.
- The Y-axis contributes the point of *here* and creation.
- The X-axis places *you* here/now to make it personal.
- The result: your own personal reality is continually being created in each and every *now* at the root chakra.

We are entering a different space within our consciousness where things we never thought of as real are becoming a little more tangible.

The Evolution of the *Now*

The *now* that is born in the root chakra does not stay there. It travels through the energetic spine acquiring more and more qualities and specifics as it goes. In each chakra along the way, it becomes more formed until it reaches the crown chakra where we experience it as our reality.

We are about to follow the *now* as it evolves through the chakras. By doing this, we cultivate each region of the energetic spine to reap its purest hue, its richest tone. Our work churns itself into loving relationships, kindness given and received, fulfilling work, laughter, inspiration. Like an invisible river flowing through the energetic spine, the *now* continuously rises. We cannot distinguish the end of one moment of *now* and the beginning of the next.

The more we pay attention to the continuity of the *now*, the more we become drawn into its vortex, deeper and deeper. Although manifested circumstances may not change instantly (my desk may still be messy, my pains may still hurt), these unwanted specifics become less meaningful and pure aliveness takes the spotlight.

What *is* simply *is* this continually changing moment. You can abide in the knowing that, wanted or unwanted, the circumstances only stay this way until they change. As you change your focus, you change your point of attraction and you change the creation of the next group of *nows* as they enter and rise and evolve into your reality. The more we realize that the *now* keeps on opening and yet remains the *now*, the more it holds our attention and the more involved in our creation we become.

In yoga, the meditative state is often compared to the flow of oil poured from one vessel to another. There is no break. It is a smooth, continuous connection. The one thing that the mind can focus on to emulate and ultimately become that state of flow is the *now*. That continuity defines the *now*.

So what does it mean for the *now* to evolve? Remember that the *now* is just a moment in time along the Z-axis. It becomes significant when crossed by a Y-axis of space to become a point of creation. Once the *here-now* has two points of view (Z and Y) it can multiply and create an entire world. It is not until it acquires an X-axis that it gains a personal self. When all this occurs at the root chakra of a human being, we have the specific conditions necessary to apply this system.

When all these conditions are met, although born perfect and complete, the *now* first begins its journey for that individual. It begins its evolution. Entering the opaque field of the mind and the even more dense material of the body, the *now* has a maze to navigate. The *now* savors the ride through you and then meets release and freedom. It then returns to the undifferentiated sea of beingness from which it came. That reemergence occurs constantly as each *now* makes its way through the tunnel of the energetic spine and reemerges at the crown chakra.

How long does it take to traverse the energetic spine and mature into a complete moment of now? No time. It takes no time because the direction of its journey is along the Y-axis. It travels where there is no time. The Y-axis' only meeting with the Z-axis of time is at its center point of *now*.

We will take as much time as you might measure on your clock to move through the next three chapters. In these chapters we follow the *now* as it travels through the remaining six chakras, but at any time in that process, if we stop to see how long it is taking, it will reliably be *now*. We remain in the continuous flow of *now*, the only moment of *flow* that can ever be experienced.

As the *now* travels up through the energetic spine, it moves through the wormhole. That means that as soon as it enters the root it is in the crown. Maybe you can say it takes eternity for it to get there. Maybe you want to call it instantaneous. Neither has any meaning. It all happens without the cooperation of time. It happens outside its borders.

The *now* may be indifferent to the content of its own journey. Or it may simply seek an alternation between adventure and peace as it streams through our vessel. Have you ever seen a child scream through an entire roller coaster ride only to run back to the end of the line to get back on for another trip? The *now* breaks into rainbow form while it wears your life. Then—poof—it is white light again waiting on line for another ride. As human beings, we ride the roller coaster, often developing such patterns of resistance along our way that we become focused on the desire for peace, ease, and a vacation in the Caribbean. Our spiritual conversations revolve around seeking inner peace, serenity, and white light. The *now*, on the other hand, is pure peace. It is made of white light and it seeks color. It comes to us for excitement. We were made for each other.

The goal of the Yoga of Alignment is to harmoniously bring you together with your flow of *now*. It aims to give *you* some relief from your suffering by introducing your intense human experience to the undifferentiated, divinely connected *now*. To be fair, it also aims to give your *now* the best ride your life has to offer, to make exquisite rainbows and soul-stirring music as the *now* glows through your being and vibrates your strings.

A Clean Slate

Although you may read this book without participating, I offer it with a more practical intention. I know that we all have areas of our lives that feel out of alignment. Financial struggles, substance abuse, addictive relationships, eating disorders, anxiety, depression, loss, physical illness, need I go on? Which one of us is free from problems? The conditions we consider to be obstacles to our joy contrast sharply with the objects of our desires. (Desire gets our full attention in the next chapter.)

But this system has nothing to do with controlling outer conditions. We have instead turned our attention to the inner garden. Does that make our work here ineffective? On the contrary. I want you to have tangible results from your efforts with this system. I want you to know without question that your inner work is measurably benefiting your life. That's why I recommend that you steep your mind in the concepts, concentrate your mind in the meditations in the Practice Section, and quiet your mind in the process. If you have been doing that up to this point, it is likely that you are finding a new joy in the present moment, and you are certainly paving a Z-axis of success and fulfillment ahead of you.

The profoundly sacred point of connection with the Infinite, the root chakra, still has one more overwhelmingly generous gift for you if you open yourself to receive it. We have already touched on it briefly. You might call this gift *forgiveness* because in its infinite compassion, it relieves you of all that you may perceive as past error or regret, but it is more than that. You might call this gift *free will* because in its infinite potential, all is possible, but it is even more than that.

The undifferentiated, unmanifested state of pure being that pours itself into form as *you* in every instant of *now* offers you an extraordinary gift. Some would call it "wholeness." Others prefer "emptiness." For our purposes they mean the same thing in that they both point to a state of existence free from distinctions. It just *is*. Let's call it its "isness."

This isness provides you with a clean slate. You have the option in every single moment to create anew, but we rarely free ourselves from the hardened templates of our past creations. We believe religiously in the habit of looking back in order to know how to move forward. In fact, it has become our policy to write each new day's script on the previous day's page, a practice that confuses, distorts and hinders the clear expression of each new inspired moment.

Ignoring the sparkling and unlimited *now*, we become prisoners of the stories we tell ourselves about conditions. The repetition of these stories keeps us locked in the past, whether it takes the form of an unwanted relationship, job, illness, or poverty.

The clean slate of the *now* gives you the key to that prison door. Once you know that you can create your new experience from scratch, you are free. Once you truly sense that you have the ability to stop acting out of your history, your wealth in the currency of life becomes unbounded. You begin drawing from the bank of all possibility and depositing into your personal creation. Once you accept the sacred offering of pure consciousness, your most material concerns reveal their spiritual nature, and your most spiritual aspirations become your reality.

We are about to move our attention up through the remaining chakras. We will watch how the perpetual creation of the *now* develops as it rises through the energetic spine. Like a slow-motion instant-replay of an imperceptible but crucial athletic moment, we will examine how your *nows* unfold into your reality.

Because of our new understanding of the mysterious inner wormhole of the energetic spine, and because of our new appreciation of the X, Y, and Z aspects within us, we can watch this unfolding from a unique and mystical perspective. In the next three chapters we trace the details of the sequential creation of the *now* as it develops through the remaining six chakras. We do this with full knowledge that this evolution of the *now* actually takes up no time and moves through no space. With this paradoxical yet logical game plan, we now set out to learn how you can participate in the creation of your reality in a way that is more satisfying, more joyful, and more aligned with your true nature.

See Session Five of the Practice Section for the experiential exercises that correspond to this chapter.

Section III
Planting the
Seed:
Bringing
Awareness to
Each Chakra

Chapter 12

The Wild Herbs

of Paradox:

Desire and Ego

As we follow the flow of life force in its ascent through the spine, it might seem natural to check in next at the second chakra and then at the third, but we will not work in that order. We are in the process of discovering the up-force hidden within gravity. If we don't approach this with clarity, the bottom two chakras might keep us in a holding pattern, bouncing us up and down, as if we were caught in a pinball machine. We are leaving the silence and stillness of the root chakra and moving into the activity of life. The main question now is, which way will we go, up or down?

Water is the element of the second chakra and water drains downward. The second chakra can be seen as a repository of all the unconscious forces and impressions you have collected over innumerable lifetimes. Its storehouse is deep and its contents mysterious. Not long after our consciousness rises from its central birthing place at the root chakra, it reaches the watery second chakra. From there it will typically sink right back down and continue in that loop unless we step in and intervene.

We have three primary reasons for doing this:

1. We are working toward building a clear channel for

life force (as the *now*) to pass through us as it rises in our spine. If the *now* gets caught in the riptide of the second chakra, the reality it will unfold will be a distortion of the true desire of our heart. We probably will not even recognize the reality we are living as having come in answer to our asking. Instead we will experience ourselves as victims of circumstance. In contrast, by discovering our buoyancy within the depths of the second chakra, we bring the path of the evolution of the *now* into alignment with our true nature. This paves the way for more good fortune to manifest in our lives as our reality unfolds.

2. We are on a spiritual expedition in search of the up-force. You may already have access to this buoyancy in your daily life. However, if you are plagued by fatigue or depression, releasing these burdensome and amplified connections with outer gravity will probably become your primary reason for doing this work. The energy and joy that become palpable once the up-force has a clear pathway to travel may just become your favorite aspect of this process.

3. We are systematically bringing awareness to all the chakras. If our consciousness gets blocked at the second chakra, it may never fully reach the higher chakras. If that happens, we will not sufficiently develop the qualities resident in those chakras and they will not have a chance to become integrated into our daily lives. By finding a safe pathway up through the draining force of the second chakra, we are opening ourselves for courage, love, clear communication, and wisdom to become part of the fabric of our personalities.

With all that in mind, we will next consider the attributes of the third chakra. Then, once we have established a stronger vortex of energy there, we will continue on to the second chakra. With the energy of the third chakra in place, when we return to the second chakra, instead of sinking, we will joyfully float on its deep waters. Here's how it works:

Fire (the element of the third chakra) moves upward. Earth (the element of the first chakra) also moves upward as support. By spending some time developing the strength of your third chakra, you can create a strong force field between the first and third chakras leading in the upward direction. Then, when we return to the waters of the second chakra, we will have a lifeguard on duty.

Weeds

Most gardeners probably don't harvest their weeds, but I do. In the spring, before my swiss chard or watermelon seeds have even germinated I gather young weeds. In a few weeks the weeds I am collecting will threaten the survival of the whole garden, but if I fill a basket of these young weeds now and cook them up for dinner, they will outshine the rest of the meal. Filled with vitamins and minerals, and more delicious than any greens I can plant and grow, the wild vegetables are the stars of the meal.

In another section of the garden I grow herbs, but the most potent of the medicinal herbs grow nowhere near my garden. They are wild. They survive with no fertilizer. They flourish with no cultivation. Nobody planted hem. In their wildness lies their strength.

Wild plants interfere with our plans. They can totally overtake the garden and turn all our efforts to chaos, but there is more to their story. If properly recognized and gathered, if respected and collected, they give us the most powerful nutrition and the most potent healing power of all that the earth has to offer.

We have a couple of similar weeds growing in the inner garden. They grow on their own with no seeding, nurturing, or watering from us. They will grow under almost any conditions and we tend to see them as problems in the spiritual garden. Desire and ego are our two major weeds and they will be the subjects of this chapter. Once we cook and tincture them, they will nurture and heal us.

Ego as Distortion

The third chakra is considered to be the home of the ego. People use the word *ego* to mean many different things. When I use it here I am talking about the notion we have of ourselves as completely separate, individual beings. Let's think of ego more as a state of consciousness than as an entity. From the point of view of the ego, it is "me against the world." " Life's journey continually threatens my survival, and I must push or be pushed, dominate or be dominated, and ultimately kill or be killed." That is the posture held by the ego.

As long as we operate exclusively from this understanding, we live in a treacherous landscape haunted by the dark side of every desire. Every duality lures us to its light while lurking in the shadows as disappointment and defeat.

This translates into a day-to-day reality of endless struggle. Every time we want to win, to be right, or to look smart, we simultaneously fear losing, being wrong, or looking stupid. Within the desire to be accepted by our peers we hold an inner fear of being shunned by them. As our attention oscillates between the desire for gain and the fear of loss, we become resonant with the vibration of ego. We merge with the state of consciousness that focuses on survival.

It may not seem like this would be very problematic. After all, we all want to survive, we want to win, and we like being right. The problem is not necessarily in the desire (as is often believed), but in the oscillation. As our mind jangles back and forth between reaching for what we want and defending against its opposite, our entire resource of awareness gets consumed. It leaves hardly a crumb of consciousness for experiencing the life force within us. It leaves us with little capacity to experience the joy of the moment, and when it comes to clearing a path for the *now* to move through us, the wildly oscillating ego pulls the *now* on a jagged pathway leaving many unhappy memories in its wake.

Ego as Instrument

We live in the light of the fiery sun (the celestial body associated with the third chakra). The light of the sun lets us see the distinctions between all things with our eyes (the sense organ of the third chakra). As we observe the boundaries between things, we can't help but notice our own separateness (the form of consciousness associated with the third chakra).

We have seen how the defensive and fearful qualities inherent in the separate consciousness of ego can create problems for us, but as is always the case, there is another side to the story. The ego stores many benefits in its bag of tricks. We just have to look for them to see how abundant they are.

Being a separate and distinct instrument gives us the thrill of focus. A specific instrument makes a specific sound. A violin sounds different from a tuba. A hammer does a different job from a drill. As you begin to see yourself more as an instrument, you can expand your appreciation of your unique talents. The specific shape and size of your mind, your energy field, and even your body become the elements of your creative potential.

Realizing this, you become conscious of yourself as a creative vortex pumping out unique realities. These realities would never have been lived had it not been for your specific perspective. The universe takes joy in this creation, and as you become aware in the process, so do you. As your creation becomes intentional, you also provide a more satisfying ride for the *now*.

The ego serves us as a motor. It is filled with energy which can either explode randomly like fireworks gone amuck, or can rocket us to the fulfillment of our most precious desires, rarely even stopping to refuel.

The more we appreciate the ego as our body, personality, and all that is separate, specific, and unique about us, the more we transform the ego from a weapon of destruction into an instrument of creation. Like a violin or a paintbrush, we become the material through which the artwork of our lives takes form. The question we will consider shortly is, "If I am the instrument, who is the artist?"

Awakening

The third chakra is all about dynamic energy, action, flame. It is alive, awake and full of power. Like the blazing of the sun that sustains life on earth, the third chakra radiates energy to the entire body keeping it healthy and vital. If you are experiencing health problems of any kind, you can be encouraged to know that your third chakra may be weak, blocked, or in some way deficient in energy. Regular meditation on this center energizes your system and supports your healing. It refills your energy reservoirs and rekindles your inner fire.

The first and second chakras operate on a completely unconscious level, but here at the third chakra, we begin the awakening process. Ideas begin to take form and manifestation pours forth from potentiality. The third chakra begins clothing the *now* in the style of your personality. Will it wear the pain and defensiveness of the disconnected ego or will it fill its small region of the universe with beauty and harmony?

The Paradox of Ego

Here is the paradox: *The ego wants all for itself, yet is happiest when involved in generous giving.* This wonderful paradox may just be the most far reaching of the gifts the ego bestows upon us. If we accept it, unwrap it, and use it in the spirit in which it is given, we find it to be the most expedient route to happiness.

In order to comprehend this paradox and make use of its gift, we will cultivate the energy of the third chakra. Your efforts here will have the effect of polishing the rough ego and making it into the great instrument it truly is. It is said that by mastering the energy of this center, you gain many powers and become free from all disease.

Developing this chakra can be seen as a two-phase process. The inner aspect is meditation. The outer aspect, which we will look at now, involves Karma Yoga, the path of selfless service.

Karma

Karma refers to actions and the consequences of those actions. Everything produces karma. Thinking, breathing, talking, seeing, hearing, eating, all the activities of your life that create movement produce karma. Even desire produces karma. Desire generates a thought, which motivates an action, which eventually leads to the fruit of that action. Every movement generates a wave. It creates a ripple effect through the universe and through time. Every wave you generate will eventually come back to you. If you want it to be a soothing, caressing wave when it reaches you again, you can begin now to generate waves that are in harmony with your true nature. Viewed from the point of view of anyone observing your behavior, these look like waves of kindness.

Because we can't *not* be active, we are always producing karma. We must breathe. Our blood must flow. Our atoms must spin.

Our senses must perceive. We are perpetual motion machines and therefore perpetual karma machines. When left to our own ego state of mind, we use our movement—mental and physical—to try to get everything we want. (Remember the first part of paradox of ego: *the ego wants all for itself.*)

Since the ego is as resistant as it is allowing, we vibrate back and forth between our many desires and our many fears of failure. This oscillation, the signature of ego, keeps us alternating between positive and negative experiences, rarely finding satisfaction, even in the fulfillment of our desires.

This is where the second half of the paradox comes in. *The ego is happiest when engaged in generous giving.* When you realize that the roller coaster ride that you have been white-knuckling through with the ego at the wheel is not satisfying, you look for an alternative. The antidote to the ills created by the conflicted ego can be found in the path that dissolves conflict and embraces the law of karma. That path, called Karma Yoga, is also called the path of action, or the path of selfless service.

Words can be so tricky. Let's get very clear about what we mean by selfless service. Another way this path is commonly described is to say that we devote all our actions to God and release all attachment to the fruits of our labors. More tricky words. Let's translate *God* as *Good* since no matter how divergently we may all conceptualize *God,* we come together in the agreement that *God* is whatever we consider to be *Good.* Next, let's translate *the fruits of our labors* as *specific outcomes.* Now, Karma Yoga becomes something more like this: I devote all my actions to the good of all (myself included) and I release attachment to the specific outcomes of my actions, knowing that good begets good. By clarifying this understanding, we can see that our highest commitment is to the Good, whatever that may be. Our interest in the specifics of the manifestation naturally takes second place to the intention that the process, the outcome, and the influence on all touched by our actions, be *Good.*

How will we know that our actions are in service of Good? How can we be sure that we are maintaining this huge intention? It will help to take our translation one step further. Abraham often reminds us of the phrase spoken by Joseph Campbell, "Follow your bliss." Let's understand the navigational strategy of devoting all your actions to good as "following your bliss."

This means that not only are we offering our actions *to* the flow of good, also, in the process, we are receiving *from* the flow of good. Not only are we offering that within us which we experience to be good, we are receiving in like kind. So here, it helps to turn our attention briefly to the aspect of receiving.

Abraham points out to us that we tend to see our good as coming through the vortex of our parents, our employers, or from whomever we are accustomed to getting all our good stuff. However, once you release your focus from the person acting as the "middle-man" between you and Source Energy, you also release all the limitations of your "middle-man." (Your parents can only give you so many toys. Your employer can only give you so much salary.) In Karma Yoga you open yourself to personal, direct access to Source Energy with its infinite resources. Now we can further translate *releasing attachment to specific outcomes* as *releasing limitations*. We now see that this applies to our offering as well as our receiving. Finally, our new interpretation of *selfless service* is: *Following your bliss with no limitations.*

If you are confused by this unconventional translation, it is probably because we have sufficiently blurred the distinction between self and other so that the words "selfish" and "selfless" have lost their meaning. All that is left is what Abraham often reminds us, "Good feels good and bad feels bad." Rather than seeing selfless service as a denial of "self," we are seeing it as an embracing of "Self."

The list of benefits associated with Karma Yoga is long. As you consider this path, you may suddenly feel like a kid in a candy store. This path offers immeasurable joy. It promises to keep you fit and healthy. Karma Yoga purifies the heart preparing you for knowledge and wisdom. It generates unity and pledges longevity. In fact, this path is said to please God.

It seems like an out, an escape from the clutches of ego. Sign me up! Wait a minute. Is this path of selfless service the most selfish path you could possibly consider? Yes, that is the gift. That is the paradox. That is the power of the third chakra.

Four Steps

Swami Sivananda says, "No meditation or samadhi (state of super consciousness) is possible without a preliminary training in karma yoga."[1] He describes four different ways of understanding the spirit of Karma Yoga. We will use these four "inner attitudes" as steps leading us into the brightly sunlit garden of the third chakra.

Equanimity

The first state we want to develop on the path of Karma Yoga is equanimity. This state has you focus on the aliveness of the moment regardless of conditions. With this inner attitude in place, you face all challenges with easiness and patience. As you serve the best interest of all, you make no distinction between prestigious work and lowly work. You are as willing to scrub toilets as you are to star in a movie. You are the same no matter what. You are balanced regardless of circumstances and conditions. Of course you will always be birthing preferences and desires as you move through life, but this state sets the background tone of balance and openness. It lays a ground that allows life energy to flow. Equanimity transforms the oscillating ego wave of elation and depression (alternating between access to and disconnection from Source) into the grounded hum of balanced joy.

The Bhagavad Gita (verse II, 38) tells us:

> *Having made pleasure and pain, gain and loss, victory and defeat the same, engage thou in battle for the sake of battle; thus thou shalt not incur sin.*[2]

This message tells us to abandon the zigzagging, dual fascination of the ego and to act with full participation in the moment. Do whatever you do as you move through life with one hundred percent commitment to that act. As in meditation, maintain unbroken awareness. Do not even stop to consider if you are winning or losing.

This process will help you "release your attachment to the fruits of your labors" as you "follow your bliss with no limitations." Remember, we are operating in the field of paradox. If you try to fall back on logic in this atmosphere, you will likely become confused. Why? If you carry the reasoning of selflessness to its logical conclusion, you will mistakenly think you must abandon all joy in the process of selflessness. If not, you may be acting from selfishness and not really "doing it right."

That selfish motivation to access joy and freedom through selfless service, the ego's mysterious urge to transcend itself so that you can achieve unwavering happiness, is its own act of Karma Yoga. It sacrifices itself by pointing you toward enlightenment. If there were nothing in it for you, would you really consider serving others? The ego moves us toward wisdom before we are wise, and yet we must be wise enough to heed its call.

> *Exercise: You will know you have lost your inner attitude of equanimity anytime you feel yourself moving in the direction of negative emotion. On Abraham's emotional scale, this would be the direction of disempowerment[3]. Catch yourself as often as possible in the fury of your disconnection and ask*

yourself the following question: Is it worth trading in my joy for this upset?

Abraham often urges us to adopt the motto, "Nothing is more important than that I feel good." On the surface, that sounds like extreme selfishness, but it is the only true path to selflessness. When you feel good you overflow with kindness toward others. Only when you feel bad can resentment and hatred take root in your consciousness.

Kindness and service also provide an instant pathway directly into feeling "good." When you adopt the attitude, "Nothing is more important than that I feel good," kindness toward others becomes your main vehicle carrying you to your goal. That is the paradox of ego. Nothing is worth trading your joy in for. The yoga of equanimity teaches us how to live that ideal.

Surrender

With the inner attitude of surrender we discover the answer to our earlier question: If I am the instrument, who is the artist? Once we adopt the inner stance of surrender it becomes obvious who the artist is. We spontaneously embrace the notion that we are only instruments in the hands of God.

To the extent that we empty ourselves of the blockages produced by our fears and defenses, we become resonant instruments for the Infinite to create through. We become God's paintbrush, God's violin, God's hands, and God's voice. Krishna's flute was just an empty reed but when Krishna played it, it produced heavenly music. As we open our central Y-axis pathway, making room for the *now* to pass through us unfettered, we become empty reeds for God's music to play through us. Our lives become radiant, vital, joy-filled.

A song by Dr. Rickie Byars-Beckwith and Rev. Dr. Michael Beckwith[4] sums up this inner attitude with beautiful music:

> *Use me, Oh God, I stand for you and here I'll abide as you show me all that I must do. Command my hands. What must they do? Command my life. It's here for you.*

In this attitude, we act for the fulfillment of divine expression. When in doubt about those expressions, work always for the benefit of all. As with the practice of equanimity, we are again releasing our grip on the fruits of our labors. If we must stop mid-project, we can easily smile and drop what we are doing without regret. If a big wave comes and dissolves our sand castle, we release it immediately. Always joyful, we act in accordance with the demands of the situation, knowing that our connection to Source is reflected in how we feel.

> *Exercise: Let anxiety be the trigger that lets you know you have lost touch with the inner attitude of surrender. Speak a prayer or affirmation of surrender. "I am an instrument of divine love." "I am an instrument of God's wisdom." "Direct my thoughts, words, and deeds for the benefit of all I encounter." Set your intention firmly. Make a commitment to service. Your anxiety will disappear.*

Gratitude

Although you may be inching toward the release of attachment to the fruits of your labors (following your bliss with no limitations), you may find it difficult to completely let go. The inner attitude of gratitude becomes tremendously useful here. It can be hard to let go of something. It is easier to replace it with something else. Gratitude replaces the expectation of results and the need to be thanked for our efforts. It acknowledges the paradox of ego in which we find ourselves.

In the state of gratitude, we devote all the fruits of our work to the divine unfolding. As we recognize that serving the whole is the greatest thing we can do for ourselves, we give thanks for the opportunity to serve.

> *Exercise: Every time someone thanks you, use that as a reminder to give thanks for the opportunity to serve. Also, when you find yourself feeling resentful or used, reframe your action as Karma Yoga and give thanks for the indicator of your disconnection. Find your way back to feeling good. Recommit your actions to the overall good (which includes you).*

Oneness

This attitude promotes the awareness that everything is Self. As you look for the divine spark in the hearts and eyes of everyone you serve, you develop a keen awareness of the oneness from which your individuality springs. You may get sudden flashes of insight informing you that there is no difference between doing something for yourself and doing something for someone else. Everyone benefits from every beneficial act. It is all one big organism.

That means that even when you serve your Self, you are serving the whole. The Yoga of Alignment offers a slightly different perspective on this aspect of service from that of the traditional yogic stance. Looking honestly at this little twist in the road will help us move through it smoothly where we might otherwise have encountered some blockage of flow.

Here is the quirk: If you serve others and don't serve yourself, too, you set yourself apart from others as having a different status. You may see yourself as one who either has more while others are needy, or who is superior while others are inferior, or who is somehow better than others and is therefore in a position to help those poor, miserable, lowly, unenlightened people. From this stance, you affirm your separateness more than your oneness.

Setting yourself apart can also land you on the other side of ego's fence. You may find yourself feeling like others are getting all the benefit while poor you are sacrificing the best years of your life thinking only about them. You feel a moral obligation to be selfless but inwardly you resent those you serve.

Both of these distortions of service (feeling superior or feeling resentful) can be easily remedied by including yourself in the sea of humanity you are serving. To the extent that you see yourself as superior to those you serve, you are not doing Karma Yoga. With your resentment toward those you serve, you negate your own hard work. In fact, resentment turns your joy *into* hard work. Karma Yoga is light work. It is following your bliss. It is serving God in the manifest world. To the extent that you cause yourself suffering in the process, you have stepped off the path.

> *Exercise: Experience how you are benefited when others are served. Share in their happiness. Allow yourself joy knowing your happiness benefits others. Feel the invisible connection between you and all beings.*

By cultivating these four states, *equanimity, surrender, gratitude, and oneness*, you will develop spiritually at an astounding rate. This is the express route. You can't lose. Your ego becomes your engine. The more your ego wants, the more you can say to it, "I know exactly how to get that. Do selfless service." You will be enthusiastically grateful every time you find an opportunity to serve. You'll be going around looking for people to help. Don't worry if you are doing this for "selfish" reasons. It is just your ego pushing you toward enlightenment. Just keep working with all four steps.

Once you taste the joy that comes from this practice, you will be going wherever something needs to be done. You will seek out those in need. If someone is hurt, you'll be there to soothe him. If someone is hungry, you'll be there with food. You'll be so happy that others will wonder what your secret is. Everything you want will come to you easily.

"Did you just say everything I want will come to me easily?" As you work with the third chakra, manifestation will come more quickly, but manifestation of what? It's time to turn our attention to the second chakra and to tincture *the paradox of desire*. We can now enter the watery maze of desire at the second chakra with cheerfulness and confidence.

The Paradox of Desire

Most spiritual and religious teachings recommend releasing all desire, but in order to do this you must desire desirelessness.

The universe is completely organized by the form of desire called attraction. Can we say the paper clip desires the magnet? Does the magnet crave the refrigerator? We take the forces of attraction and repulsion into the very personal realm of feeling when we call them *desire*. These attractive forces constantly move everything, and yet we only tend to call them *desires* when they move *us*. If we take a leap here and choose to understand all attraction as desire, then we could say that our physical universe is based on the energy of desire. Desire is the glue that holds it all together.

Then we can see that the desire we experience as human beings fills only one tiny realm of the universe of desire. Gravity, magnetism, orbit patterns, molecular interactions, the integrity of the entire physical reality that we depend on to be consistent moment after moment, all this owes its reliability to the all pervasive desire that moves everything.

In an effort to avoid disappointment, rejection, and loss, we sometimes decide to give up all desires. When we do this, we step out of harmony with our own nature, which is desire. We set ourselves apart from the rhythm of the rest of creation. This may seem contrary to many widely respected approaches to the subject of desire. It is not as different as it seems. If the path of *desirelessness* is taking you where you want to go, then it is fulfilling your unspoken *desire*. You are successfully moving through the paradox.

If however, you are on a path that advocates renouncing all desires and you are encountering great obstacles, then you might be caught in the paradox. If you feel like you are running around in circles, if you feel depressed or lethargic, if you feel jammed up, frustrated or angry, you have probably gotten tangled in this web. Going deeper into the subject of desire might just lead you out of your conundrum and into the open space that you seek.

With a little open-minded examination, we may find that the path of *desire* and the path of *desirelessness* turn out to be the same path.

At the second chakra, desires begin tugging on the shiny new *now* that just emerged at the root chakra. The moon (the celestial body of the second chakra) has its own force of gravity. That gravitational force tugs on the earth's great bodies of water (the element of the second chakra) creating the tides. Similarly, desires pull on your ascending *now* creating a tide in your reality. The ebb and flow of events in your life may seem random and externally ordained, but much of what you see around you is the direct result of your energetic relationship with your own desires.

Desire as Delusion

The first part of the paradox of desire reminds us that "most spiritual and religious teachings recommend releasing all desire." They must have a good reason for doing this. Desire takes us out of the moment and projects us into the future. It creates a judgment that *what is,* is inferior to what *isn't.* It keeps us ever grabbing at what we don't have and ever dissatisfied with what we do have. Desire leads us to believe that our satisfaction will come in externals via a future that never arrives. It keeps us out of our experience and in a deadened place of expectation. When our desires are unfulfilled we are unhappy. When they are fulfilled they do not have the power to make us happy. Their promise of fulfillment keeps us deluded and we continue on and on in ignorance and pain.

No wonder we are advised to leave it all behind. Desire is extremely problematic and seems to be deceiving us, leading us down the wrong road, but like a sticky piece of paper that you can't get off your shoe, desire is not so easily discarded. You may step on it with your other foot, but that only moves it from one shoe to the other. You pull it off with your hand and it sticks to your hand. You pull the paper off your right hand with your left hand, and now it is stuck to your left hand. It just won't go.

Desire is like that, but it is more subtle and we are more easily fooled by it. We may think we are finally free of it, but it is stuck to our back like a "kick me" sign. As soon as you decide to work towards releasing desire, you land squarely in the second part of the paradox, because in order to release desire, you must *desire desirelessness.* The minute you declare you are giving up desire, you are smack in the middle of a new desire. That piece of paper is sticking to you again.

Fluid Desire

There are two main ways to approach this dilemma. One is to proceed with the renunciation of desires but from a perspective broad enough to include the paradox. If you can manage not to get tangled in the language of it, and you can live with the apparent contradiction, then the traditional paths to enlightenment will serve you well, but I have seen many people depressed and lost in this paradox without understanding why. They are so committed and sincere that they have attempted to give up all desire and the swirling drain of the second chakra tugs at their spirit. What would have been an uplifting spiritual practice has become a heavy burden to bear.

In between the creative fountain of infinite *nows* gushing through the first chakra and the blazing power of the sun at the third chakra, lie the deep waters of desire that steer our vessel, whether we are conscious of them or not. We don't usually identify these desires. We wait until they have formed into comprehensible outer cravings.

I want the fastest computer. I want the biggest house. I want the shiniest red tricycle. I want a raise. I want some ice cream. I want a vacation. All the wants like these that we can articulate as discrete items do not live at the second chakra. The second chakra is fluid, malleable, it holds the *feeling* of the desire. All it wants is satisfaction. The form that it takes is irrelevant. Once you want a red sports car or a green pickup truck, your desire has advanced beyond the primal sea of attraction filling the region of the sacrum and pubic bone.

The desire that lives in the second chakra has much to do with relationship. Freshly individuated from the universal oneness, the personal consciousness seeks reconnection. It desires wholeness. When it seeks that connection along the Y-axis, it looks upward to God. When it seeks connection along the Z-axis, it becomes sensitive to attractions and seeks a mate. When focused on the X-axis, it looks to integrate different aspects of the personality to reach a sense of wholeness.

When free from obstructions and imbued with love, the desires of the second chakra lead to a spiritual knowing of the divine, loving personal relationships, and self-acceptance.

Is Desire Good or Bad?

You don't have to go far. You can leaf through just about any book on the philosophy of yoga and you will quickly find instructions on recognizing desire as the enemy and eradicating it. If you delve a little further, you will find a surprising goal that motivates much of the practice of yoga.

The physical postures, chanting, meditation, and study all point toward leaving this human experience and never coming back. The ultimate goal of hopping off the wheel of birth and death, getting out of the rat race of suffering (synonymous with the human experience) seems strange to our Western minds. We *like* life. Yet if we steep ourselves in the yogic shape of mind, many of us soon experience one of two things.

Either we find ourselves embroiled in inner conflict, drawn magnetically to the wisdom and precision of the path of yoga, yet slamming on the breaks as we realize we are racing at full speed toward the edge of a cliff. Or we demand of our Western consciousness an alchemical shift that may or may not authentically occur within us.

Prem Prakash reframes this dilemma in a refreshingly positive light:

> *"Yoga in the West is taking a form contrary to the world-negating view that has developed in India. And this may be the West's gift to the yogic tradition. The yoga of the next millennium will, in my opinion, provide aspirants with philosophies and practices that will enable them to be both citizens and yogis, to be in the world but not of it."*[5]

The practices recommended here as the Yoga of Alignment arise from the same intention. If successful, they will further this prediction of a new option within yoga, one that will allow you to move passionately forward with your practice while staying true to your reverence for life and its processes. At the base of all of those life processes we find desire.

Duality

The singular, discrete increment of the infinite oneness that entered your being at the root chakra divides at the second chakra. Here, just like the first division of the zygote in the physical uterus, the one becomes two. Duality is born and the force of desire instantly takes hold. Positive and negative, male and female, black and white, up and down, all explode into existence. It is no wonder that desire, the attractive force itself, a mere corollary of duality, gets passionately labeled both good and bad.

Within the argument between those embracing desire and those renouncing it, we find another level of paradox. You will hear impassioned speakers claiming diametrically opposed "truths" about the nature of desire and offering opposite recommendations regarding what you should do about it. What is important about all this, from our standpoint, is the paradoxical nature of the argument. Before we start taking sides and jumping on soapboxes, let's see the trap and move past it rather than falling into it.

Desire is not good or bad. It is the force field generated *between* good and bad. Desire is the magnetism between the north and south poles of the magnet. To relegate desire to one side of any duality would be analogous to calling magnetism a phenomenon of only the north poles of magnets and not south poles. Desire is a product of the world of duality in which we find ourselves. Trying to rid ourselves of its influence would be as futile as the north pole of a magnet attempting to remain unaffected when in the presence of a south pole.

Ironically, whether the magnet desires its opposite pole or it desires transcendent freedom from its own magnetism, in either case the fulfillment of its desire would be the same: oneness, wholeness, neutrality. The same is true for us. Our desires pull us toward that which we believe will complete us. We look for satisfaction which will, at least momentarily, bring us to peace, fulfillment, contentment. Whether we embrace desire or attempt to rid ourselves of its influence, in either case, our desire is the same. We want wholeness. We seek the oneness from which we came.

What Do We Do About Desire?

Attraction to the object of our desires finds its least subtle proponent at the second chakra. The sexual and reproductive organs associated with this chakra provide a home base for desire in the energy body. The Z-axis of time, also associated with these organs, is paved by desire. Because desire is still so new at this center, we find here an uncommon opportunity to harmonize ourselves with the essence of our desires.

The word *yoga* is derived from the Sanskrit root *yuj*, meaning to join, to unite. Yoga, in all its varied methods, is really the science of uniting. It offers different paths suitable to different personality types. Whether the practitioner practices physical postures, breathing, philosophy, or devotion, the person practicing yoga is acting on a powerful desire. It is the desire of the individual for the Absolute, the human seeking the Divine, the finite desiring the Infinite. In yoga, the innate desire for reconnection and wholeness gets directed to the Y-axis.

But desire also moves us forever along the Z-axis. This relationship between desire and the Z-axis is the subject of much controversy on the spiritual path. It is considered acceptable and even valuable spiritually to channel your desire toward God via the Y-axis, but once your senses are pulling you forward along the Z-axis, your desires are thought to impair your spiritual practice. That's why vows of celibacy, poverty, and asceticism top the pyramids of many spiritual paths.

In this system we are looking to harmonize the characteristics of each chakra for the most joyful and fulfilling life experience we can unfold. As the *now* passes through the second chakra, it becomes vitalized with desire. What are we going to do about it?

The simplest way to rise out of the quicksand of the delusional aspect of desire is to unconditionally appreciate it. Appreciate every phase of desire. Enjoy the birthing of the desire. Enjoy the feeling of incompletion and magnetism. Enjoy the force field of attraction. Enjoy the activities and decision-making, the coincidences and synchronicities, all the circumstances that fill the time and space of your desire. Enjoy the sense of approaching fulfillment. Enjoy the completion. Enjoy the momentary lack of attraction after fulfillment. Enjoy the birth of new desire. Enjoy each phase so authentically that you would be happy to stay in any phase of the process forever. Another paradox.

Whether your desires are material or spiritual, the same method applies. That means if you are saving to buy a house, and it seems hopeless and futile because you have so little money, then we can safely say you are not enjoying the magnetism. If a material desire seems unattainable, yet you can't seem to stop desiring it (and don't want to), enjoy the flow of time within the magnetism of it. Feel how good it is to be in its field of attraction. Realize that as soon as you get the house you will have new desires that will be unfulfilled. Realize that now, as you wish you had a house, you are steeped in the fulfilled desires of the past, many of which are no longer interesting to you. This is how it goes, on and on.

Some will get depressed at the picture I am painting. That is because they have not spent enough time in the third chakra material. Once you have practiced devoting the fruits of your labors to the divine unfolding, once you have developed equanimity, understanding that gain and loss are truly equivalent (all that matters is the experience you bring to the moment), once you understand the oneness of all beings and are perpetually grateful, you blissfully ride the rapids of your desires enjoying the extraordinary scenery as you go, thrilled at the ride, happy to rest at the end of the day, and eager to ride again tomorrow. Do you own your new house yet? Yes or no, there will be joys and challenges in either phase. Neither is good, neither is bad, they are different flavors of *now*. The one consistent ingredient in both is desire. Abraham says,

> *"We want to help you understand the preciousness of the unfulfilled desire. If you could, in this moment, begin to feel appreciation for the fact that the desire exists, and feel anticipation about its unfolding, rather than instant disappointment that it has not manifested, your energy would clear up by 95%. And your manifestations would begin to flow to you so much more easily."*

Well, it would seem that this is very much like giving up desires. No, it is the opposite. You become like a surfer, riding the desires. Then you are grateful for the desire. You are not so attached to the outcome or fulfillment of any one desire but you love the strong current that comes to you as powerful life force. If you fall off your surfboard, you may get more enmeshed in resistant patterns blocking the flow of the desire. Hop back on and let the waves carry you again.

This sounds less like how to get a house and more like how to be happy even though you don't have a house. It turns out these two are the same. There is an old story that I have heard in several versions. Basically, an enlightened being strolls through the forest. He first passes an ascetic yogi. The yogi who has spent years upon years, in fact has devoted his entire life to the path of discipline and renunciation, who has been meditating 23 hours a day and eating close to nothing, whose bones are stretching through his skin, asks, "How far am I from enlightenment?" When the answer comes, "Three more lifetimes," he throws a fit of discontent.

The enlightened being continues on and comes upon a simple servant who prays and meditates in his spare time. His understanding is childlike and he is happy to meet the great enlightened master. "How many more lifetimes before I become enlightened?" The enlightened being points to a huge tree with thousands and thousands of leaves. "As many as there are leaves on that tree," comes the answer. The simple man becomes so overjoyed to know that he will ever achieve his goal that he becomes absorbed in the ecstatic state of the master and reaches enlightenment in that instant.

More simply, Abraham has said, "If you could feel good about not being in the flow, you'd be in the flow." Desire and desirelessness are starting to look so much alike, I can't tell one from the other. When you resist desire, you can get very depressed. By *resisting* it, I mean either saying it's bad or not believing its fulfillment is possible. Telling your friends that you will never be able to afford the new house or new car is resisting desire. Telling yourself you will never meet a new love is resistance, too. By being attached to a desire I mean caring when and how it comes to you. Attachment is really just another form of resistance. By *appreciating* desire, I mean loving the fact that you are a magnet living in field of paperclips of all different sizes, shapes, and colors, just waiting for you to turn your attractive field in their direction.

So, whether your desires are material or spiritual, physical or emotional, or of any other category you want to name, when you enjoy them, you become more alive. No matter what phase of a desire you may find your self in, by enjoying it, you bring yourself directly into the *now*, the only time there is. You land squarely at the intersection of the Y and Z-axes, which is the font of creation. And what better place than this point of *now* to create that which you desire?

Abraham says of the *now:*

> *"Here is the most significant thing that we want to give you about the subject of time. There is only this powerful now. Doesn't matter if you are physically focused or whether you are non-physically focused, everything is happening 'now.' Which*

means, now is when we perceive; now is when we interact; now - everything is happening now."[6]

Tantra, the yogic path of ecstasy, takes this approach to desire. Georg Feuerstein describes the Tantric ideal regarding our relationship to desire. He says:

> *"The enlightened being, however, floats in the infinity of all desires and therefore does not have to cling to any one desire but can remain in the world, at peace, fulfilled, unattached, and yet at the same time with a relish for life in all its countless forms."*[7]

Time is Made of Desire

We are not the only ones seeking completion through desire. From a certain perspective, we could say the whole universe is involved in the same pursuit. Here is one way to imagine it.

If you've seen a film lately, you watched the light pouring out of a movie projector, hitting the screen, and revealing patterns of shape, color, and movement that translate into meaning for you. When we go to the movies, our minds get involved in the story. Our emotions take hold. The screen usually goes unnoticed, but if the light had no screen to stop it, we would have no movie to watch.

The exact moment when the light hits the screen resembles a single moment of *now*. It marks the transformation from potential to experiential reality. Once the movie begins, we are immediately swept up into its world.

The *now* creates a similar effect. Let's picture a universe filled with infinitely small, highly charged ping-pong balls. These ping-pong balls can be thought of as the ancestors of electricity. They carry a charge reminiscent of positive and negative, but these attractive and repulsive forces are more ancient, more abstract, and less linear than their electric descendents. They contain worlds of relationship within their charged potential.

Imagine the universe as a sea of these ping-pong balls, randomly moving about, pushed and pulled by the attractions and repulsions between them. Now imagine your attention as a light projecting along your Z-axis. Like a movie projector, it shines in a certain direction, vitalizing the ping-pong balls that it falls upon. It heightens their attractive forces so intensely that they collide into each other with tremendous force and, in an explosion of neutralization, they become a reality.

The desire between these ping-pong balls culminates in their merging and neutralization. This becomes your personal *now* as you place your attention in a certain direction. Of course, this does not end with one creation of one *now*. It continues like an endless cascade of neutralization moving ever forward, producing the effect we call reality. Once we can perceive it, it is over. The charge has been consumed and the next wave of attraction, explosion, neutralization, and perception is underway.

Because this happens in a steady flow of *nows*, we don't perceive the mechanics that produce the illusion. When we are watching a movie, we have no awareness of the sprockets on the projector or the thickness or thinness of the film. We accept the effect. We go along for the ride, the romance, the adventure, the mystery, without feeling the need to dismantle the projector in order to understand it.

If we don't even do that with a movie, why would we attempt it with the awesome *now*? Because it gives us something we need. It reveals the role of desire in the creation of our reality. I don't just mean your desire for an ice-cream cone or a sports car or world peace. It is not your personal desire that is at the basis of all this. It is the desire that holds the planets in place. It is the desire that holds the molecules in place so that vanilla ice-cream doesn't suddenly turn into mint chocolate chip.

We begin to realize that what we perceive as empty space is really dense with potential realities. The space right in front of you is filled with innumerable charged "particles" just waiting to burst forth as your reality. As you shine your Z-axis upon them, they merge in neutralization and completely occupy your awareness with their finished product, distracting you from the next force of attraction, just below the surface, about to become your reality.

So it is these two levels of desire that combine to create your experience. The desire of the universe for itself, and the desire born in you, demonstrated by where you put your attention.

Like Attracts Like

There is a universal law called Law of Attraction. Abraham describes it in this way: "That which is like unto itself is drawn." Ernest Holmes says, "Since we are thinking beings and cannot stop thinking, and since Creative Mind receives our thought and cannot stop creating, It must always be creating something for us. What it will make depends wholly upon what we are thinking, and what we shall attract will depend upon that on which our thoughts dwell."

That means that the nature of your vibration as you are shining the light of your attention will only vibrate charged ping-pong balls of a like nature. They will in turn merge and neutralize to create more realities like the one you are living. The more we open the pathway for the life force to pass through us unimpeded, the more we vibrate in harmony with our true desires. As our desires become pure, we manifest realities that please us.

Law of Attraction, which causes things of a like vibration to be drawn together, acts equally in all directions. We will move more deeply into all of this in Chapter 17. For now, it will serve you to simply understand that the more you can match your desire, the faster it will come to you. We will soon see that the Z-axis can actually become a sort of wormhole, just like the Y-axis. The Z-axis wormhole connects you with an as yet unmanifested reality. As you become so similar in vibration to the object of your desire that you and it are like middle C being played on two different pianos, the notes will become indistinguishable and that which you desire will manifest in your reality.

Special Effects

As you understand desire as a producer of time, then you can create a wonderful effect by directing your desire upward along the Y-axis. This would normally be called seeking spiritual awareness. When you "look up" in this way, you are superimposing the forward limb of your Z-axis (time/desire) onto the upward portion of your Y-axis. Two things happen as a result:

1. You add time to your otherwise timeless Y-axis. This has the paradoxical effect of accelerating your perceived spiritual journey. (I say perceived because from the perspective of the Y-axis, there is no journey. You are already there.) Introducing the perspective of time (Z) to the Y-axis gives the impression that your *now* travels more "quickly" on its timeless evolution through your spine. This raises your vibration.
2. With the same act you also *remove* time from the Z-axis of your worldly desires through the influence of the timeless Y-axis. Without time separating you from the fulfillment of your desires, manifestation becomes instant.

This all happens to the degree that you stay present at the intersection of the Y and Z-axes. If you move forward or backward on the Z-axis, by leaning toward the past or future, you lose your presence in the *now* and remove yourself from the font of creation. If you move up or down on the Y-axis, you come to different chakras and different degrees of evolution of the *now*. Although each chakra has a related desire, here at the second chakra, desire is still close to its source. It has not fully differentiated into a desire for a specific thing. Like a baby reaching for a rattle, it will take anything interesting that you give it and make that its full object of attention. What will you give it?

Tantra

In among the different paths of yoga that attempt to vanquish all desire, we find one school of thought that studies and embraces desire. Tantra recognizes the paradox of desire. This path, rather than asking you to transcend your desires, invites you to move through them with awareness, intention, and spiritual devotion.

Of the infinite dualities born at the second chakra, Tantra focuses much attention on the pair of opposites that can be described as static vs. dynamic energy, or still vs. moving, or unmanifest vs. manifest. This distinction translates into the language we have been developing as the Y-axis (the still, static, all pervasive consciousness) and the Z-axis (the dynamic, creative movement through time).

The alternating separation and reuniting of these two states (still and dynamic) continually births reality in a cycle of creation, preservation, and destruction. Or in the wording of Swami Niranjanananda Saraswati, Generating – Organizing – Destroying (G-O-D). It patterns an expanding and contracting throb in the universe that exists in both microcosm and macrocosm. Desire is the force that keeps this play in motion. Tantra prescribes many ways of finding your resonance within the macrocosm and bringing forth your divine nature.

When you link your unending desires (pulling you forward on the Z-axis) with an awareness of your divine spark (accessible through the Y-axis) you bring light into the material world. You fill your senses with all the commotion of the Z-axis without having your consciousness leave the Y-axis.

What's so different about that? Most of us get so distracted by the activities of life that our attention is almost exclusively in the past or future. This habit removes the experience of the divine from our activities and leaves us with the empty feeling that life has lost its meaning or value.

Instead of completely withdrawing our attention from the senses and their Z-axis journey in order to focus on spirit, the path of Tantra assures us that within the Z-axis of time, desire, and the senses, we can rise exactly as we wish through the Y-axis. We can experience the union we seek. The finite can meet the Infinite. The human being can find God.

What Do You Want?

Whatever you want, that is the subject of your life. It keeps changing but it never stops pulling you. Like a carrot dangling in front of a racehorse, our desires steer us. They set our direction and our speed as we trek along on our Z-axis. When we really want something, we run toward it. When we are lukewarm about it, we mosey along, easily swayed toward another desire.

Abraham often poses the question, "Have you come to appreciate the contrast of your time and place?"

Contrast is born for us here at the second chakra where it is easy to appreciate. It is easy to appreciate, because it has no value judgment yet. It is mostly variety. It is red and blue, fast and slow, hot and cold. We tend not to notice it until it evolves further and becomes good and bad, wanted and unwanted. Then we don't appreciate it so much anymore.

Bringing the second chakra into alignment so that it can receive an abundant flow of life force means embracing desire. Embracing desire means maintaining your upright posture on the Y-axis while feeling the gentle breeze of time reminding you that you are alive and moving forward. It means looking forward to that which you desire while savoring the magnetism of its unfulfillment (or fulfillment) in your *now*.

Meditation

To many, ego and desire seem like weeds in the inner garden. The insidious destructiveness of these wild forces prevents them from manifesting the fruitful life they want. By looking deeply into these weeds, we are finding them to be potent healers, herbs of great abundance and great value.

So far we have been engaging our conscious mind in the process of transforming these potentially sabotaging forces into assets. Now we will go deeper by engaging the second and third chakras in meditation. The meditations in session seven of the Practice Section are simple. They are purifying. They can change your life.

We have begun to understand desire's relationship to the second chakra and ego's relationship to the third. In an effort to benefit from these seemingly problematic aspects of our nature we have shifted our notion of these tendencies from a sense of pesky weeds to one of medicinal herbs. We have begun to heal ourselves, to make ourselves whole through our new understanding of these influences. Now, we can take that healing deeper through the purification of these two energy centers in meditation.

See Session Six of the Practice Section for the experiential exercises
that correspond to this chapter.

Chapter Notes

[1] Swami Sivananda, *Karma Yoga* (India: The Divine Life Society, 1985) page 13

[2] Swami Sivananda, *The Bhagavad Gita* (India: The Divine Life Society, 1995) verse II, 38 page 36 Special thanks to Vyaas Houston for deep insight into this verse. More information at www.americansanskrit.com

[3] For a full explanation of Abraham's emotional scale, read *Ask and it is Given* by Esther and Jerry Hicks (The Teachings of Abraham) (California: Hay House, 2004)

[4] You can listen to the song *Use Me* on Rickie Byars-Beckwith's album *I Found a Deeper Love* and on the *Agape Chant Anthology*. You'll find this and much more at www.rickiebyars.com For more information about Rev. Michael Beckwith and Agape, visit www.agapelive.com

[5] Prem Prakash, *The Yoga of Spiritual Devotion* (Rochester, Vermont: Inner Traditions International, 1998) pages x-xi

[6] Abraham-Hicks Workshop Recording, Seattle, WA 6/28/03 Tape 4

[7] Georg Feuerstein, *Tantra: The Path of Ecstasy* (Boston, Massachusetts: Shambhala Publications, 1998) page 229

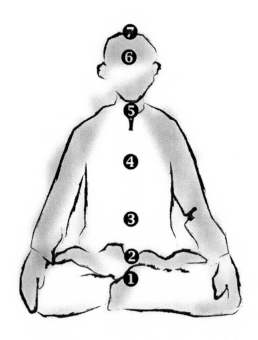

Chapter 13

Wild Flowers:

The Heart

That Sings

L ove is not like other things. Living in a vibration of love can totally transform everything in your life. Its mystical presence has the power to soften all resistance and bring forward the best in you. It calls toward you the most harmonious aspects in others. It attracts favorable circumstances. Love vitalizes your essence because it is the fundamental substance of the universe, and when you activate it in your awareness, you see things truly. Your perspective becomes bright and you understand life through your heart.

In order to bring greater love into your vibratory mix, tend to the *now* as it ascends on its journey within your energetic spine. Pay particular attention as it rises from the fiery center of the abdomen into the garden of the heart. The quality of the *now*'s journey profoundly colors your life experience. It forms your personality and directs the unfolding of your life.

The *now* traverses the diaphragm, rising above the pelvis and abdomen (in no-time) and immediately feels the gentle breeze and open air of the garden of the heart. Here, your eternally evolving moment of *now* encounters one of the most valuable products of root, leaf, and stem. Here, it beholds the heavenly flower of love.

Tending to the *now* as it unfolds itself as love, you become love[1]. Then, no matter what you are doing, or thinking, or saying, you are doing it as love. The *now* becomes infused with the presence of love so that no matter what other subject may be enjoying the spotlight, the light itself is made of love.

Silence

"Anahata," the Sanskrit name for the heart chakra, means "unstricken." Like a guitar string patiently waiting for a player, like a silent drum, like the vocal chords at rest, the love in the heart is unspoken, unworded. It simply, silently is.

As the name of the chakra suggests, the love we are capable of experiencing far exceeds our ability to describe it in words. We usually send flowers, with their deep silent message, to put our point across. Of course, the inadequacy of the word doesn't stop us from trying. There is no book large enough to hold all the love songs we've composed, generation after generation. But a song is a little different. Here's why.

Song

Love rises. It is so attuned with the Y-axis that it floats up and right at its next stop it meets its most cherished partner, the voice. With the alchemical merger of love and voice, the impossible becomes possible. We sing about love, and through that singing, love is communicated.

Since love so often finds expression through song, we reflect on the heart and throat chakras together as a unit. From this perspective, you can care for some of the nooks and crannies in the garden of love that typically go untended. Here you can cultivate not only a deeper sense of love, but also dignity, honesty, confidence, and freedom.

Although love can take on many forms, and although scores of human motivations are associated with love, here we focus mainly on the essential love that sits at the center of all love. It exists always, everywhere. It is available to all beings in every situation. It transcends circumstances and it needs nothing.

Similar to your relationship with life force itself, you have only to open to love's presence. Abraham says, "All of you would feel fantastic love oozing out of you all of the time were it not for your resistance of it, because your natural state is that. Your natural state is the state of pure positive emotion. That is who you are."[2]

In this process, you have been carrying your awareness through the energetic spine, clearing your path and opening yourself to the flow of life force as you go. You have been paving the way for the *now* to evolve creatively through you. As you continue to cleanse and align the energetic spine in the fourth and fifth chakras, you tune your instrument for the expression of love as sound.

You saw how the *now* is born in you at the root chakra. In the same way that your access to infinite, undifferentiated life force takes root at the perineum, so does your production of word and sound. Let's return for a minute to the root chakra to see where all love songs begin their journey.

Sound Rises

Love rises to find its singing partner, the voice, and it reaches down to its roots to find its song. All vocalizing begins at the root chakra.[3]

The Root of Sound

That same central point of the perineum, which we examined so thoroughly in our exploration of the X, Y, and Z-axes, also sources sound. In the same way that you are rooted in the Infinite, the unmanifest, the center of the universe, you are similarly rooted in primal sound, often described as *Om*. This level of sound is called "divine voice" because it is the sound the universe makes all on its own. It has no form. It is just sound. This primordial, undifferentiated sound manifests as *prana* or the energy of the universe, and you interface with this energy through breath. Of course this sound does not sit still. As soon as it meets with a human energy system like yours, it rises into the energetic spine and begins its journey. Just like the *now*, it evolves along its way.

The Seed of Sound

When the sound arrives at the third chakra, it evolves to a seed thought. At this stage it becomes somewhat differentiated from the great hum of the universe, but still remains abstract. It is like an apple seed which doesn't look, smell, or taste like an apple yet, but contains all "appleness" within it. At the third chakra, the sound is the same in all languages. It may ultimately rise to expression in English or Spanish, but in the belly it is all the same. It even crosses the species barrier. Here at the third chakra, this silent phase of sound is the same for you, Fido, and Fluffy. For this reason, you and your pet communicate more from this center than through the language-focused voice.

You can use this awareness to more consciously communicate with your furry, scaled, and feathered friends. At the third chakra, the form of the sound might have color and shape, but it has not yet developed to the level of verbal language. It's an abstract tendency that you can sense. You may not know exactly what it is yet, but it has narrowed itself down, and it is on its way to becoming something other than a cosmic hum.

From the Heart

As the sound energy rises to the heart, the senses get involved. This stage, at the fourth chakra, is called the intermediate, unexpressed stage of sound. Here it comes very close to being expressed but still remains "unstricken." At the heart center, the silent sound gets feeling. The more you allow your heart to be filled with love, the richer your voice becomes when the sound emerges at the throat. Speaking from the heart means letting the sound marinate in the fourth chakra before it bursts into form. It means opening the energetic spine so that the flow of sound from the root to the throat stays fluid, rhythmic, and becomes enriched as it passes through each stage of development, particularly at the heart. Singing from the heart requires a steady source of universal sound flowing from the root. From there, all it needs is a fluid journey to the throat center where it makes beautiful music.

I Hear You

At the throat chakra you arrive at articulate expression. The sound has completed its journey from its root and emerges victorious as, "Hi, how ya doin'?" or whatever else you have to say. Everything you speak travels this pathway. Every word that leaves your mouth originated in the cosmic hum that entered your unique human vortex at the root of your torso. As you turn your attention to this ongoing process you may find a dramatic shift in your unconscious word selection and in the timbre of your voice.

The Love Cycle

The partnership between the heart and throat centers is the bond between love and expression. They are mutually beneficial. Without its song, the heart's love remains muted. Without love to express, the throat becomes a vocal automaton. As sound cycles through the 4th and 5th chakras it creates a secondary wheel of energy which includes the spins of both chakras individually.

Chaitanya Kabir reveals the nature of this cycle saying, "When we sing, the voice vibrates the body, reaching the ear. The ear receives and passes on the sound wave – especially higher frequencies – feeding energy to the brain, helping the mind relax. As this happens, the focus drops from the mind to the heart. The heart expands, inspires the voice, and the cycle begins again."[4]

The joy of love in the fourth chakra (heart) flowers as song in the fifth (throat). It is no coincidence that the yogic path of love and devotion, Bhakti Yoga, presents a long-standing tradition of chanting and singing. Even in pop culture, love finds its most compelling expression in song. Working with these two chakras opens your heart to the expansive presence of love, and frees your voice for its authentic expression. Nothing elevates the spirit more purely than love. Nothing heals more completely than love.

As love rises from the heart into the voice, you speak or sing. The utterance of sound from your throat brings the internal energy of your inner garden out into the open. As it flows from your mouth, it divides and follows 2 separate pathways:

- One pathway leads back into your inner garden via your ears (The ears are the sense organ associated with the throat chakra.).
- The other pathway leads to the inner aspect of those others who hear you with *their* ears.

If your voice flowed only outward, we might simply call it a stream, but that's not the case. It flows back in through your ears before you can even close your mouth. As your ears participate in this process, they bend this stream into a cycle.

Whether your voice enters your own ears or those of another, its next stop is the heart. (Notice the word *heart* has the words *hear* and *ear* in it.) The sound of your voice flows in through the ears and back to the heart influencing the utterance of the next sound.

Listening With Your Heart

It is possible to turn up the volume on this cycle and to gather many benefits in the process. The garden of the heart overflows with color when you practice conscious listening. That is, listening with your heart.

Listening to Yourself

Spend a minute or two visualizing the pathway that your voice takes as it rises from your heart, expresses in your throat, exits your mouth as vocalized love, re-enters through your ears and returns to your heart to seamlessly begin another round. Chanting, mantra, prayer, and affirmation practices maximize the power of this sacred cycle. Take another moment to see your pure words as they swirl and multiply in the fertile gardens of the hearts of the others who lend an ear. This gives you an inkling of the power you wield with your words, your tone, and the inflection of your voice.

Listening to Others

Now take a moment to visualize someone else speaking or singing. The sound pours forth from deep within her and immediately enters both your ears and hers. Rather than listening to the words for content or information, let your chest become relaxed and open. Just as you understand how food enters the body through the mouth and travels downward to the stomach, imagine the sound coming in through the ears and flowing down to the heart chakra. There, instead of deciphering and analyzing it, you feel your friend's voice.

Your conscious mind will still do its listening automatically. You simply shift your perspective from being one with the mind to becoming a listener seated in the heart. You may notice your mind always chomping at the bit, trying to interrupt, urgently wanting to speak its part. From your new perspective, you won't feel so compelled to act on that urge. You become interested in the enjoyment of listening.

Listening with your heart provides a deeper satisfaction than the higher pitched activity of the mind's style of listening. But don't worry. You will not shut off your mind in this process. In fact, your mind functions more accurately, more compassionately, and as we will see in the next section, when you do respond, you speak more in accordance with your inner truth. Even though your attention rests on the feeling of the speaker's voice in your heart, you understand what she is saying as usual and you respond appropriately.

She won't even realize you are doing this, but from your perspective there will be a noticeable difference in your experience. You begin hearing much more than you may be accustomed to hearing. Your heart now hears the speaker's heart. It senses what is unspoken, unstricken. Heart to heart, you hear between the sound waves, and you know much more than the meaning of the spoken words.

A certain amount of this type of listening goes on automatically. It can be called natural listening since it is built right into you. However, since many of us have forged defenses around our hearts, we have hardened this chakra and shunted all our listening up to the head. Still, you may be one of the rare few who practices this soft art of listening. If this is the case, by adding this conscious dimension to your already cultivated ability, you fine tune and take greater enjoyment in your loved ones. Which brings me to a couple of big questions.

What effect does listening from the heart have on your relationships and of what personal benefit is this practice to you? Allowing your heart to sense the message sent from the heart of another via the voice brings your hearts into greater communication. You more finely attune your language to each other. With your hearts in primary communication, you use your voice and language as tools rather than as the primary communicators. This adds depth, richness, and expanded awareness to your relationship.

In practical terms, this can translate into less arguments, less judging, less conflict, and more mutually satisfying solutions to seeming problems. On the positive side, it can mean more spontaneous expressions of appreciation. It means more time spent laughing. It cultivates intimacy and trust. It also begins to melt away the hard walls that have kept your heart separate from your love. The reunion of these two parts of the whole leads to unimaginable healing. As they reunite, the joy is indescribable. You may just start singing.

It doesn't matter if you are the only one in the conversation who is doing this. You don't have to say a word about it. See if new dimensions start opening within your relationships.

Speaking From the Heart

When you speak from the heart your inner garden brightens. The resonance created between your heart and the flow of its expression can inspire you to say things that will amaze you. You will hear the words coming out of your mouth and think, "Wow! Did I say that?" Unlike the more common experience when speaking from the head, "Uh oh. Did I just say that?" Do you know that feeling? The words fly out of your mouth and before you can catch them, it's too late. You may immediately regret saying what you just said, but your heart and the hearts of others have already received the comment. Then you spend a whole lot of words trying to cover up, make excuses for, and explain away your mis-spoken words. At this point we dig ourselves in deeper, adding more and more energy to the initial undesirable vibration of our head-words. At any point in this mess you can switch gears and begin speaking from the heart. Good things will come of it.

It doesn't matter whether you are asking your boss for a raise, tucking in your children at night, giving a campaign speech, or asking your mate to take out the garbage. Speaking from the heart raises the vibration of that interaction and makes it more fully what you want it to be. The pathway doesn't change although its expression may range from gently hummed lullabies to booming oration. As the sound rises freely from the heart, it evolves into its most useful and appropriate form for that situation. It reflects in word, tone, and music the message of your inner being.

The ability to communicate clearly and with compassion comes from opening the channel between the heart and the voice. With this practice, life force flows smoothly through the energetic spine from the heart chakra to the throat chakra. When this pure form of communication flows naturally, it is usually labeled *talent*.

There is another major benefit built into this process. It is such an intrinsic part of the speaking mechanism that the two cannot be separated. It is always at work whether you are speaking from your heart or not. Whether you are amazing yourself with your wise words or constantly removing your foot from your mouth, this remains true: your words are creative. The words you speak are not just pieces of information you pass around. They are seeds you plant. They live on once they fall from your tree and they grow where they land. They land in the gardens of the hearts of all who hear—and that includes you. They then form their own seeds and live on for generations and generations spreading from heart to heart as they travel on the winds of words.

The more you speak from the heart, the more you plant seeds that beautify and enrich your inner garden. The more you keep your heart defended and speak only from your mind, the more time you spend pulling the weeds seeded by your mis-spoken words. Now you can see how easy it is to shift this, even mid-word.

Gratitude

Imagine a manuscript of your life. It has everything written in it. Everything you experience, how it all feels to you, what every cell in your body is doing at every moment, the direction of spin of every one of your electrons, every detail that could possibly be said about what is going on with you is written in this manuscript. And now, in the infinite number of ongoing inscriptions entered into this document, you turn your conscious attention to one specific event and say, "I love *that*. *That* is one of my favorite parts."

Have you ever seen a page that has a certain phrase circled, underlined, highlighted, and then has arrows all around it pointing to it? When your eye glances at that page you cannot help but look at that phrase. Your eye goes right to it. It is an irresistible force.

You are in the process of co-creating your next moment. You steer your life, intentionally or unconsciously, in whatever direction you place your attention. By expressing gratitude for the things that you love in your life, you underline and circle them in that great big book in the sky. You grab the attention of the universe's fulfillment committee. You employ the irresistible force. With your gratitude, you are paving the way for the next moment to have more of that. Little by little, the manuscript of your life gets filled with these circles and arrows and keeps multiplying their fulfillment.

So when you speak gratitude, be aware of it rising from your root, becoming enriched with feeling in your heart, acquiring voice in the throat, sounding in your mouth and getting strengthened by you hearing it. If you have the good fortune to be heard by other sympathetic, supportive souls, these people become loudspeakers for your gratitude. They vibrate with the request for more of this in your life. If you are looking for ways to serve others, as we discussed in the section on Karma Yoga, listen for others' expressions of gratitude and let it pour into your heart. Resonate with their gratitude and allow yourself to serve as a vibrational amplifier for more good to come to them.

What is Your Heart's Desire?

What is the difference between the heart's desire and all other desires? The heart's desire aligns harmoniously with every aspect of you. Whatever you want in such a pure way that no matter where you hold it, no matter in what mood you think of it, no matter where you place it in your body, no matter from what aspect of your life you view it, it is unconflicted, that is your heart's desire. If you don't know your heart's desire, it may be your heart's desire to know your heart's desire.

The throat chakra means "pure." Speaking the truth of your heart, your words come through clean and truthful. By opening this pathway, you express your heart's desire with every sound you make. Speaking from the heart is a practice of purification. It is an opportunity to purify your language so that your speaking becomes a true messenger of the heart.

Let's not forget that the heart chakra functions in the open air (its element). The garden of this chakra lives as springtime year round in the heart. Here, the rainbow display of flowers delights beyond reason. In those intoxicating moments of spring when the colors of the physical world briefly expose their nature as pure light, we seem to fall in love, over and over again, almost in spite of ourselves. This is the heart's desire.

Rising through the energetic spine into the realm of air brings freedom. Freedom is another aspect of the heart's desire. Once in touch with this freedom, you blossom into the greatest version of yourself. You discover your freedom to move. This liberation of movement invites love into awareness. Love uplifts like nothing else. It resets your alignment with the Y-axis.

The most immediate entry point into this reality is in the air around you. We are just like the fish who don't recognize the water. We don't know that we have freedom. Once we realize it, or even desire it, we sing.

The movement liberated in the heart chakra rises into expression as song. Love can't help but sing. Freedom blows through your instrument and your life becomes its music. As you speak, your words are made of the movements of your heart. You can discover a perpetual current of life deep within you, hidden inside the partnership between the heart and throat chakras.

With this partnership strengthened, and the heart's desire consistently spoken, you attract to you that which you love. You communicate more authentically, creating a space of love and appreciation in your relationships. You speak with honesty, clarity, and authority, paving the way for good works and expanded success. Your words match your inner truth, sending clear messages into the universal creative medium to deliver to you that which you truly desire. Confidence and dignity resound in your voice. The meditations and exercises in the Practice Section can assist you in this enriching practice.

We have combined our understanding of the heart and throat chakras in a way that removes the sentimental excess from our notion of love and gives the voice a significant role in our spiritual lives. How you use your voice, what words you say, the pitch and tone of your sounds, all these choices reverberate in you and in others. You can let them flow on at their habitual setting, probably doing neither major good nor harm, or you can bring some added interest to this process. By paying attention to the flow of energy to and from your heart, you can enhance your life, empower yourself, and heal many inner conflicts. This is how the garden flowers.

See Session Seven of the Practice Section for the experiential exercises that correspond to this chapter.

Chapter Notes

[1] To cultivate a sense of *being love*, visit the Affirmative Contemplation website and practice with the YOFA™ *I Am Love* meditation recordings. www.AffirmativeContemplation.com

[2] For more information about the teachings of Abraham, visit www.abraham-hicks.com

[3] Swami Sivananda describes the four stages of sound in his book, *Kundalini Yoga* (India: The Divine Life Society, 1994) page ix

[4] Chaitanya Kabir, *Divine Singing Songbook* (Boulder Colorado: Sounds True, 1997) page 3

Chapter 14

Expansive

Perspective:

Wisdom and

Mastery

Opening the first ripe watermelon of the garden is one of my great joys in life. How does that red, sweet fruit come from the dense muddy soil? I become like a child, absolutely amazed, every time. With dirt on my arms, carrying the pristine, sparkling fruit, I come as close as I can to holding wisdom in my hands.

With the first fruit of the season, we taste the sweetness of life. Swami Sivananda tells us, "Instead of counting the numbers of leaves in a tree, try to eat the fruit directly. Try to enjoy the eternal bliss of the Self by direct realization. This is wisdom."

The opening of the sixth and seventh chakras marks the arrival of wisdom. Here, we can transcend the illusion that we are separate from each other. We are about to explore how the sixth chakra, also called the third eye, and the seventh chakra, also called the crown chakra, sharpen your intuition and guide you to act in accordance with your highest intentions. Peering out at life from the broadness of perspective offered by these higher chakras heightens your awareness of your connection to all others.

You will find that your efforts bear fruit similar to the bounty of a well-tended garden. Practicing the meditations in the Practice

Section will lead to the wisdom, empowerment, confidence, and peace of mind that come from inner knowing. Once the energetic spine has been aligned and these higher chakras awakened, you can trust your spontaneous actions to be beneficial. Your words become helpful to others. You act with compassion. You are better able to deal with all that comes your way.

In the physical world, if someone throws you a ball quickly, you don't have to plan your response. The brain sends messages through the proper nerves to the appropriate muscles so your immediate reaction to the fast approaching ball is to catch it. In a split second, the brain orchestrates your response and your body follows with precision. Similarly, when confronted with a challenging situation, these higher chakras instantly assess the nature of the situation. They funnel energy to the necessary chakras and inspire action born of wisdom. By practicing the Yoga of Alignment meditations on a regular basis, we establish a clear pathway for broader intelligence to flow through the energetic spine. This allows wisdom to express through us more purely in every newly created *now*. We act with unified intention that carries the power of our whole being with every move. Life becomes clearer, brighter, and more joyful.

It Is In You

Seekers of wisdom often travel far and wide, craving the knowledge that they believe will set them free. Many practice rigorous rituals in an effort to develop wisdom. These efforts may bear fruit or they may not.

In this system, we will take a simple approach. You know that no matter how far you travel, the wisdom you seek travels with you. It started the journey as fully present within you as it was when you thrilled on foreign shores. The purpose of the quest was never to find wisdom outside yourself as first assumed. The purpose has always been to reveal it within you.

Wisdom is calm and it is good. It is content and it is eager. It is flexible and it is enthusiastic. Check its credentials. If what you have found is driven by compulsion or dissatisfied in the present moment, it may not be wisdom at all. Pema Chödrön says:

> *Maybe the reason there are Dharma talks and books is just to encourage us to understand this simple teaching: all the wisdom about how we cause ourselves to suffer and all the wisdom about how joyful and vast and uncomplicated our minds are—these two things, the understanding of what we might call neurosis and the wisdom of unconditioned, unbiased truth—can only be found in our own experience.*[1]

Similarly, Abraham often reminds us that, "Words don't teach. Only experience teaches." You may believe that you must develop wisdom by adding information to your mind. We will approach this more as a process of clearing away the old mental patterns to reveal the natural state of wisdom that is innately yours. Rather than developing wisdom, you find it. You retrieve it from deep within yourself. Once it bursts into your awareness, you merge with it. You become it. Your life begins to paint wisdom with you as its brush. The pattern you trace with your footsteps becomes invisible art. The trail of your words leads others to themselves.

Wisdom Written is Knowledge

Wisdom cannot be written because it is ever flowing. It must be lived. In its written, stagnant form it is knowledge. It was wisdom in the one who lived and wrote it. On the page, it is knowledge. It can reconstitute itself in you if you take the knowledge and spark it in your own consciousness. When it ignites your own wisdom, what was written crumbles away and you become living wisdom.

You may codify it again in your own language and pass it along as more knowledge, but only when it lights someone else's candle will it again live as wisdom in that person. Wisdom is alive. Let's look at some knowledge and see if we can light ourselves with its flint.

Two Become One

The 6th chakra, or third eye, brings the two eyes of the physical body to unity as a single energetic eye between and above the two physical eyes. This begins the reversal of duality that was birthed at the second chakra.

In chiropractic, we talk about a phenomenon known as the Lovett relationship or Lovett Brothers[2]. This approach reveals the relationship between the top bone of the spine with the bottom bone. It continues to associate the second bone from the top with the second bone from the bottom, and so on. Understanding these relationships helps us understand how the bones tend to move out of place in patterns and how we can more efficiently correct them.

We already explored the intimate relationship between the top and bottom chakras in Chapter 10. I even did my best to convince you that the root and crown were identical. One way to look at the top and bottom of our energetic spine would be to imagine two funnel shaped vortices with their openings at the outer chakras (1st and 7th) and their narrow end at the inner chakras (2nd and 6th). Looking at these two pairs of chakras in this way makes a lot of sense when we see them as functional units. Both open to the Infinite; both lead into the individual.

We can go further and understand the 6th chakra to be in a Lovett type relationship with the second chakra. Remember, we progressed from the undifferentiated cosmic unity at the root chakra to the birthing of duality at the 2nd. Here at the 6th chakra the dualities reunite in preparation for their reemergence into the oneness of the universe at the crown chakra. The 2nd and 6th chakras balance and reverse each other. By continually splitting into 2 and reuniting into one, they keep the play of life in a pattern of alternation between form and no form. They keep our sense of reality fresh and new by imperceptibly creating, disassembling, and recreating it.

Understanding the relationship between the 2nd and 6th chakras helps us flow more smoothly through life. The broader perspective offered by the 6th chakra helps align the desires of the sacrum with the greater whole and moves us to act on our desires with wisdom. In the same way that the 6th chakra benefits the 2nd, the 2nd chakra also benefits the 6th. The sacral chakra has the effect of keeping our wisdom grounded in our humanness. This encourages compassion and flexibility.

One Two Three: Om

At the center of the two-petaled lotus between the eyebrows we find the well-known vibration of "Om." This is the mantra of the 6th chakra. Om is a sacred syllable that is a name of God, the supreme reality, the absolute. Its sound is the human rendition of the cosmic undifferentiated hum of the universe. Meditation on this sound is said to lift the spirit to transcend the finite world of individual, separate consciousness. It brings the individual into unity with the All. This union is the goal of yoga.

The 6th chakra not only brings the duality of "twoness" to the unity of "oneness," it also addresses the trinities. It most clearly manifests its "threeness" in its association with the syllable "Om" which is alternately spelled "Aum." (The Sanskrit symbol for Om also looks much like our numeral 3.)

The three-letter spelling, Aum, gives us a much better picture of the trinities encoded in this sacred utterance. Each of the three sounds included in the syllable, Aum, represents a quality and an aspect of God, and as we will see, resonates primarily with one of the axes.

A

This sound is made by letting the mouth hang gently open and allowing the most primitive sound to come forth from the throat. In English it sounds like "uh" as in the word *up*. The "A" also leads us "up" the energetic spine because this first letter resonates with the Y-axis. "A" represents the timeless vertical, the spiritual component of our human journey. Just as we saw that the Y-axis holds us steadfast in the *now*, the "A" portion of Aum attunes us to the present moment.

The Upanishads, sacred texts of yogic wisdom, tell us the "A" represents God's wakeful stage. "A" represents creation. In the Hindu trinity it corresponds to Brahma, the creator. It is no coincidence that the alphabet begins with "A." The mingling of these occurrences of "A" as a primary force implies the all pervasiveness of God and directs us to turn first to God in praise and prayer. We do this most directly through the Y-axis.

U

This sound travels from the back of the throat through the front of the forward-thrust lips. If you could see the trail of this sound, it would trace the Z-axis within the mouth. This "oo" sound, as in the English word *do*, encompasses the continuity and "doingness" of life. It represents the journey.

According to the Upanishads, this second letter represents God's dreaming phase. "U" represents preservation through the Z-axis of time and in the Hindu trinity corresponds to Vishnu, the sustainer.

M

There is much vibration in the head caused by the sound "M." With the lips closed they outline the X-axis representing self, and the sound "M" can be found in the English word *me*.

The letter "M" stands for matter, measure, material. It resounds with the finite within the Infinite. The Upanishads call this the profound sleep state of God and it corresponds to Maheswara or Siva, the destroyer of ignorance.

Recitation of Aum can be done out loud or silently. If your mind is very busy, sounding the word helps diffuse the chatter. Generate the sound at the root, let it rise to the navel, and allow it to gain deep feeling at the heart before the "M" vibrates at the top of the head. Feel it in every part of your body. Swami Sivananda tells us that chanting Om with vigor "produces one-pointedness of mind," and brings the mind "in tune with the Infinite."

Once the mind quiets down, silent repetition is said to be most potent. If your mind is still running around, direct it to the meanings of the sounds. Use up your mind's urge to activity by giving your attention to each aspect of the trinity as you chant. This reels in your scattered energy and brings it closer to your center of *here-now*.

Realization of each of the sounds within Aum is said to bring different gifts. Realizing the "A" aspect of God brings the fulfillment of all desires. Attuning with "U" allows you to become wise and harmonious. "M" is said to bring knowledge of the physical and spiritual sciences.

There is also a fourth and silent stage of Aum, which corresponds to the unknowable aspect of God. It cannot be perceived by the physical senses and yet it is the destiny of all. It is supreme bliss. By realizing this aspect, you are said to enter the universal spirit and experience ultimate liberation.

Arriving at Now

The 6th and 7th chakras function together as the culmination of the timeless journey taken by each moment of *now* as it rises through your energetic spine. Here, each frame of your reality-movie hits the screen and becomes perceptible. Of course, this all occurs along the Y-axis, which offers us the paradox of no-time. That means that when the *now* finally reaches its destination, it is *now* just like it was when it first entered the root chakra so many chapters ago. No time has passed. It all happened in the wormhole between the root and crown chakras in one blast of neutralization, one crashing of light on the screen, one big bang in the universe of your consciousness. However, you don't experience it as a blast, a crash, or a big bang because each *now* is preceded and followed by bursts of equal intensity. This unending parade creates a fluid, uninterrupted sense of self, of reality, and of normalcy.

We are ready to bring our conscious awareness directly to this seat of wisdom. Rather than taking the long route through the chakras, rather than engaging with all the intermediate stages, we are up to the plunge. We are on the high diving board. We are looking out from the mountaintop. We are shifting our perspective to one of transcendence.

A funny thing happens up here in the heights of your consciousness. Maybe it's the thinness of the air up here, but people start acting differently. No longer solely identified with their own personal drama and the issues of ego survival, these people slide into an expansive identity. Abraham talks about blending your awareness as a physically focused being with the broader, eternal awareness of your inner being. Jnana Yoga, the path of knowledge and wisdom, advises us to leave behind our small identity and meditate upon our oneness with the transcendent Self or Atman. We only need to move gently toward this realization in order for our perception of ourselves and others to undergo a radical shift.

Who Am I?

I am filled with identities. I may think I am my body, my mind, my work, my successes, my failures, my station relative to others (parent, child, friend, mate, etc.). All these "I" portions of who I am fall into the limited category of who I am as a separate being. Each one is defined by a different set of borders. My body has its physical skin as the line between me and not me. My mind takes a more subtle approach since it has no physical definition. It forms opinions and with them makes its boundaries energetically "hard" so that there can be no confusion between me and not me.

All of these limiting ideas of who we are create the effect of funneling our day-to-day reality into a tiny corner of the infinite expanse of consciousness. The result can be frustration, boredom, a sense of tedium, and many other negative feelings of limitation. Most of us spend much of our lives and most of our psychic energy constructing these circumscribed definitions of who we are. I am a good wife. I am a high school teacher. I am a vegetarian. I am a dog-lover. I am a spiritual person. I am old. I am young. I am a bad dancer. I am a good cook. I am an artist. I am a hard worker. I am the kind of person who…

These definitions don't pop up out of nowhere. We hone them. We are constantly refining them. Like a white-bearded old whittler, sitting on the porch, whittlin' and whittlin', we keep carving out our sense of ourselves. While this is not altogether a bad thing to do, we tend to go about it in a way that shuts us down rather than opens us up to joyful living. Pretty soon the big beautiful branch we started whittling is reduced to a toothpick.

Since we *do* have bodies and since we *do* have separate perspectives in consciousness, we really don't need to do anything to affirm our separateness. It is obvious to us on all levels, physical and non-physical. The more we put our attention on it, guard it, describe it, latch on to its momentary manifestations as if they were law, the more we diminish ourselves. That is, we limit the expression of our true Self, our divine spark, our inner magnificence.

So what can we do about this? Once we can trust that our little individual self won't disappear, we can move on to the more satisfying occupation of affirming our identity with the true Self. As we begin this process, we find that not only does our individual identity stick around, it flourishes. Our thoughts become clearer, our insights more penetrating, our work more effective, our art more satisfying, our relationships more harmonious. Life actually gets better.

Swami Sivananda says, "What is to be achieved is destruction of the sense of separateness. When this is accomplished, liberation is easily obtained."[3] Meditation on attributes of the transcendent Self serves to shift the balance away from a consciousness invested in separateness. To move in this direction, you can use phrases in your meditation that affirm your oneness with the absolute. These statements clear away the constrictions that have been preventing your happiness from rising into your experience. Once there is a little space, the best in you emerges. Your experience of life becomes completely transformed.

Hilda, in her message from the nonphysical Master, Hilarion, states:

> *"What you have been seeking has been with you always.*
> *In the moment of realization, all form drops away and you*

are a vibrant part of the Light of Love, forevermore to dwell in this feeling of oneness. Then you can speak with conviction and say I AM THAT I AM, and know the meaning of Eternal Life and Immortality. Then, and then only, you realize that you have been before time began, and will be forever. You are spaceless, timeless, eternal.[4]

Who Are They?

We are not the only ones who seem separate. As you look around you will see all the other people who have bodies, names and other limiting identifiers. If you and I are infinite, eternal consciousness, what do you suppose your next-door neighbor is? We are urged to realize the oneness of the Self, not only as our own true Self, but also as the truth in all. This doesn't mean I am one infinite eternal Self, you're another infinite eternal Self, and your next-door neighbor is yet another infinite eternal Self. It means we are all one great big Self. The wisdom locked in the knowing of our oneness, once extracted by your living awareness, becomes transformational. As we saw in Chapter 2, the Upanishads tell us:

Whoever sees all beings in the Self, and the Self in all beings, that person loses all hate and fear.[5]

To develop this awareness, you can do this simple yet highly challenging exercise. As each new person comes into your awareness, whether it be a stranger or your own mother, a friend or an enemy, someone who agrees with this notion or not, choose to see this person as an extension of the Self. This person is a unique, living, breathing personalization of the One Self.

Once you see yourself in all others and all others in yourself, how can you consider hurting another? How happy will you be when you see another's success? How far will you go to sweeten the experience of another? How important will the joy you bring to others become to you?

Where Do We Go From Here?

All through this system, we have been following the flow of energy of the Y-axis in the upward direction. This may have seemed strange to you at different moments. After all, we usually look *up* to God and the beneficent forces of the universe, not *down*. Why have we been watching life force rise from below us rather than flow down to us from heaven?

This up-down motion is one of the oscillations that keep us alive, physical, and in what we know of as reality. We've been focusing on the upward flow because the buoyancy or the up-force provided by this half of the oscillation is of supreme value to us. We depend on it. Without it we are heavy, tired, limp, exhausted. With it we are leaping, laughing, loving, and creative.

Now that we have reached the crown, the only thing left to do is to return to the root. We have completed the journey from root to fruit only to discover that the fruit's main purpose in life is to make the seed for the new root. So down we go to begin again. Since we have begun to clear and cleanse the energetic spine, as we reenter the increasing density of the elements, from ether, to air, to fire, to water, to earth, we have a smoother more harmonious experience. This return can be seen as the divine descending from the heavens into the human experience.

Unlike our familiar experience in the physical world, this descent bears no resemblance to the sinking, dropping, weightiness of gravity. Instead it moves elegantly, weightlessly, like a graceful dancer, defying gravity while moving toward the earth.

It passes through each element to plant the new seed in the earth foundation of the perineum. The next rise will bring a new adventure, and as we continually develop the qualities of the chakras and align the energetic spine, both the journeys up and down, and their fruits, will become more and more satisfying. It's a good idea to pause here and remember that this up-down oscillation happens in the no-time dimension of every tiny, imperceptible, eternal instant of now.

See Session Eight of the Practice Section for the experiential
exercises that correspond to this chapter.

Chapter Notes

[1] Pema Chödrön, *When Things Fall Apart* (Boston Massachusetts: Shambhala Publications, 1997) page 73

[2] For a full explanation of the Lovett Brother relationship, consult *Applied Kinesiology Volume 1: Basic Procedures and Muscle Testing* by David S. Walther, D.C. (Pueblo, Colorado: Systems DC, 1981) pages 67-68

[3] Swami Sivananda, *Vedanta (Jnana Yoga)* (India: Divine Life Society, 1987) pages 322-3

[4] Master Hilarion (through Hilda Charlton) The Golden Quest (Lake Hill, New York: Golden Quest) page 26

[5] This is another translation of Verse 6 of The Isopanishad. The same message is also conveyed in the Sixth Discourse of the Bhagavad Gita (VI-29 & 30)

Section IV

Joyful and Abundant

Harvest: Living in the

Garden of Life

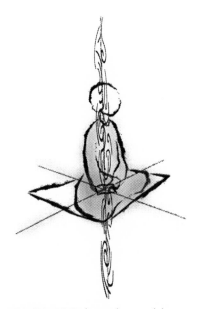

Chapter 15

Alignment

for Spiritual

Purification

We have been diligent and thorough in our exploration of the energetic spine and it is about to pay off. In a sense we have been housecleaning. The method we have used to bring our attention to each chakra in meditation acts as a powerful cleanser and scrub brush. And what are we exposing as we clear the clutter and confusion of our habitual vibrational patterns? The glowing jewels of our inner nature that have always been there.

Maybe you have already begun to get a glimmer of your own perpetual and brilliantly glowing creativity. You may have seen some sparkles of your heart's true desire. It is possible that you have uncovered the great value of being an uplifter to others. And what about the overflowing abundance of divine love, the joy of pure self-expression, and the inner peace afforded by transcendental wisdom? Have you caught a glimpse of your true nature?

These are the divine attributes, which breathe inside of you, that we are cultivating in this process of alignment. You can say we are dusting off your vitality, clearing the cobwebs that have been tangling up your joy. Now the sun can glisten on your well-polished spirit and break into rainbows in every birthing of *now*.

In addition to housecleaning, we have also been in a process of awakening. We have been rousing our innate divine qualities from their slumber. As each chakra lights up within you, you begin a further process of empowerment that lifts your spirit, strengthens your body, and sweetens your life experience.

How can these simple meditations, with the chakras as our focus, do all this? Since these qualities already reside within you, they only need to be revealed. When this happens we feel it as a re-awakening. The chakra meditations act as tuning devices that align the elements of your inner life with the greater whole. They allow you to zoom in on the essence of such qualities as love and wisdom right at the point where your non-physical spirit sings in unison with your physical body. By bringing your undiluted awareness to these points in meditation, you invite life force into these multi-directional centers we call the chakras. Vitality can then easily pour into every aspect of your life along the three axes: spirituality (Y), balance (X), and life experience (Z).

Spiritual Alignment

Spiritual alignment lies at the core of this system, at the heart of all healing, and at the source of the enjoyment of all success. You may be thinking that this cannot be true since many people who seem quite the opposite of spiritual enjoy robust health and lavish success while seeming saints can go penniless, grow ill, suffer, and die. Let's face this apparent contradiction head on so that we can move forward in our practice with confidence and sureness.

Abraham tells us over and over that we live in a universe of contrast. Every subject is two subjects: that which is wanted and lack of it. This system of aligning the energetic spine doesn't aim to control conditions with such a tight grip that we strangle life into compliance with our desires. Quite the opposite. We trust the all goodness of God as the default truth of the universe and our experience. We release and open to allow that goodness to flow into our lives. This does not mean that there won't be challenges. It means that as we move through them we exercise our divine qualities, we shine our light, glow our love, and act from wisdom in the process of living through the wanted and the unwanted.

Abraham also tells us you can't get it wrong and you never get it done. This means you lose, you win, you get sick, you get better. It is all in flux, we are always course correcting, always navigating.

This brings us to the only thing that really matters, that is the reality you are birthing at this moment of the eternal *now*. And how do you go about birthing *nows* that fulfill the desires of your heart? By having your entire being, in its physical and non-physical aspects, come into harmony with your inner truth.

You can do this incrementally by energetically aligning with your creativity, your true desires, your vitality, divine love, pure self-expression, and wisdom. Sound familiar? Yes, these were the station stops on the local train we just took up the energetic spine.

Bringing your entire self into alignment with your inner truth requires that you look only at your own life when moving through this system. Look deep into your own life, your consciousness, your beingness. As you explore the intricacies of the alignment process you may find a complexity within you of seemingly infinite measure. You will also find a lone and simple presence that effortlessly holds it all together. When you put your attention there, on your pure aliveness, your inner being, your transcendental consciousness, then everything falls into place gracefully. No matter how long your story gets, and no matter how many different thoughts and feelings you may have, find within you the one clear essence that is always *here now*.

With this perspective, let's return to the idea of those who may seem to you to be unspiritual and yet enjoying great success in life. Since there is no way to know the complexity of someone else's inner life and the nature of their alignment, it is a useless exercise to judge the value of this system by your distorted view of their experience, "saint" or "sinner." I do, however, invite you to use this system with yourself as a sacred playground and a scientific laboratory. If this work brings you closer to joy, love, and inner peace, then it is a good place to play and your research will prove these truths within the only valid arena: your own life.

Revisiting the Y-axis

We are ready to bring our focus to the Y-axis for the express purpose of staying connected to God. If the word *God* brings up resistance in you due to your experiences in the world, you may prefer the feeling aroused by the words *Universal All, Divine Consciousness,* or *Unconditional Love.* Words are powerful, so please find ones that create resonance within you with the divine qualities we are cultivating. This is not a religious pursuit. It is a purely personal exploration of your own true essence. As we do this, we promote spiritual purification and upliftment.

Since the vertical Y-axis that runs directly through the energetic spine is invisible, it may seem like an abstract idea to you at this point, like an interesting concept. That is a good place to begin. As you work with the meditations in the workbook on a regular basis, this Y axis will become more palpable in your experience. In the same way that you recognize your friend by her face or her voice, you will come to know the feeling of buoyancy that arises when you are increasing your vibrational attunement with the Y-axis. Your posture will get straighter as if your muscles are being pulled upward rather than grappling in their usual battle with gravity.

Some people have a tendency to tilt forward as they walk. It is as if they can't get where they are going fast enough. Others tend to have a concave, backward leaning stance. Still others vacillate between these two distortions with their mood. These tendencies will neutralize with attunement with the Y-axis. Those postures that shift us forward or backward from the central rod of the Y-axis lead our consciousness away from the *now* and rob us of our power which we have only in the *now*. By allowing our attention to the vertical to correct these postural habits, we empower ourselves creatively.

We have already seen that creativity begins at the root chakra at the central point where all axes meet, the point of *here-now*. The unformed *now* enters our individual consciousness at this point and begins its journey in the creation of our next experience of reality. We ease the flow through this point by aligning well above it. With this alignment, we bring ourselves more fully into the *now*. With our consciousness well centered on the Y-axis and our body likewise clicked onto the vertical, we become a very harmonious system of life.

From Fatigue to Energy

From Lethargy to Enthusiasm

From Depression to Joy

In addition to the uplifting energetic qualities resident in the Y-axis, we also find our old friends, fatigue, lethargy, and depression. I use the word "friends" because these states, although negative, are useful indicators. When we feel these personal shades of gravity such as boredom, heaviness, a sense of giving up, a feeling of "It's too hard," "Why bother?" or "It's not worth it," we can know one thing to be true. These weighty states tell us that we are dwelling too much in the outer realm of the Y-axis (the realm ruled by gravity). We have lost our ground in the inner realm of the Y-axis (the one where the up-force runs the show).

What does that mean? It means that the vertical aspect of our consciousness has slipped out of alignment with the energetic spine (or vice versa). You can imagine this axis of your consciousness to be like the pole you hold onto when riding a horse on a carousel. It does its job best when it stays centered and vertical. No matter how the horse moves and no matter how many times you go around in circles, it remains vertical and strong. If the pole tilts, bends, or leaves the horse completely, your ride may not be quite as smooth as you would like it to be.

When the vertical aspect of your consciousness gets off the track of the vertical, it disturbs your energetic spine. You then lose touch with the mystical properties within that spine. This reduces your access to the force that glides your spirit upward, that lifts your body through muscle strength, and that gives you energy and enthusiasm. Instead, like Alice in Wonderland, your Y-axis consciousness encounters the bizarre outer world where "what goes up must come down." This is quite shocking and disturbing for a spiritual axis whose nature is joy, light, and "upness."

So if we find ourselves depressed, how did we get into this predicament and what can we do about it? Our "expulsion" from the gloriously Edenesque garden of the Y-axis is really a momentary thing. We glide in and out of alignment continuously and that adaptability is the journey, the navigation process. We start calling it depression when we become fixed in this state of misalignment and can't seem to shift back into the groove. But up until this point we have not had this language of energetic spinal alignment to describe the process of depression and to implement its correction. There are many ways to talk about depression and many different models can be used in an attempt to understand it. The one we work with in this method is very practical and it helps us to regain our access to our native land, the Y-axis consciousness, the one that goes up. We will apply the energetic remedy for this in the Practice Section when we begin directly aligning the Y-axis in meditation.

An Honest Mistake

When you get caught in the downward pull of gravity, it's pretty natural to reach for something to pull you back up. We've all done it. And we've probably all also tried tugging on the Z-axis as a lifeline to get us out of the quicksand of our depression.

The Z-axis has things like food, sex, drugs, cars, jewelry, vacations, clothing, many enticements that will pull us out of our lethargy and get us moving. We peer out at our Z-axis through our desire-binoculars and find something that feels really, really good. We get all excited about it. Our energy starts moving. Activity replaces the lethargy, optimism starts to shine through, the depression even starts to seem a little silly from the point of view of our newfound enthusiasm.

There is only one problem. We are using the Z-axis to do a Y-axis job. Said another way, we are making arrangements to be pulled forward (rather than up) in an attempt to battle with the mighty down aspect of the Y-axis. We are like water skiers being pulled by the motorboat of our desire—a desire for some material thing or some sensual experience. But if we actually get the thing we desire, then it no longer pulls us and we start to sink again. So we quickly get out our desire-binoculars to look for another desire. It's got to be a good one, one we really, really want, or we won't be able to get back up on our skis.

This use of the Z-axis has given desire a very bad reputation in many schools of mysticism. They teach us that desires just lead to dissatisfaction. Once you get something, you want more. You know the story. Most books on yoga go to great lengths to portray desire as the problem and to elucidate methods for its eradication. That makes sense since traditional yoga is a spiritual practice and is a Y-axis based system. It looks uncompromisingly inward and denies all else. In the Yoga of Alignment, however, we are seeking a healthy balance between the three axes and their metaphysical counterparts. That's why we embrace and celebrate desire. Natural desire. These manufactured desires, however, sought out to lift us from our lethargy, can be trouble. Actually, it's not the desire that is the problem, but our misuse of it that gets us into all kinds of unwanted situations.

We become addicted to whatever pulls us the strongest and the fastest, but since the real antidote to gravity is not in the Z-axis, these desires, once fulfilled, cannot give us what we are looking for. They cannot lift us from our depression. Ironically, they only serve us while they are *unfulfilled*.

The only way the fulfillment of one of these desires can be as satisfying as we thought it would be is if the Y-axis component is already in place. That means we are present in the *now* to experience the moment. It means the energetic spine is clicked firmly onto the Y-axis. It means we don't *need* the fulfillment of our desire. We just prefer it. We want it. We desire it. We fly towards it. We are not looking for it to rescue us from our gloomy state.

We will explore desire and manifestation more thoroughly in Chapter 17 when we begin aligning the Z-axis. But until the Y-axis is connected to source energy, we'd be wasting our time. It would be like hiring a contractor to install a luxurious new Jacuzzi when your home has no access to water. It is that important to align the Y-axis first if we want source energy to flow into our lives. This way we are lifted by the Infinite rather than pulled forward by finite things. Let's establish our access first.

Up, Please

By entering the Y-axis, we get pulled up. And in the same way that you may develop your muscles by working out at the gym, you can develop strength in your Y-axis by aligning it in meditation. As your energetic spine becomes more magnetized to the Y-axis, you can withstand greater distractions and still hold your vertical awareness. You can experience more stressful conditions and remain cheerful and optimistic. In the face of even major upheavals, you can maintain your access to the divine, and act from creativity, power, love, compassion, pure self-expression, and wisdom. As we will explore more when we look at the Z-axis, by maintaining a good Y-axis alignment, you will attract to you more and more harmonious situations. In other words, you will have less and less stresses and upheavals in which to test your Y-axis. You will have more and more enjoyable occasions to let it shine.

We are about to begin the Y-axis meditations in the Practice Section. Once we develop a relationship with the up-force, then we can move forward by choice. We can approach the Z-axis with honor. We can move toward what we love. This is true freedom. Unfettered by the tyranny of using desires for survival we can enter the ecstasy of enjoying desires as creative celebrations.

Intention

We have been using the pre-meditation checklist throughout this program. Setting your intention, the second item on the list, now takes on a more specific role as we align the axes in meditation. As you begin to develop a personal relationship with each axis, your various intentions will reveal their primary orientation. Every desire born within you will have the majority of its momentum running along one of the three axes.

The intentions of the Y-axis are purely spiritual. They involve no cars, houses, or other material possessions. They spurt upward like springs rising from the earth, like trees pointing upward to the heavens. These desires are for connection with God, the Infinite, the all Good, the all Knowing, the Omnipresence.

Y-axis intentions are not about how to attract a mate or your relationship with your mother or your kids, or any relationship other than the one you have with your Self and with God. It is not your relationship with your religious organization or your religious leaders, either. Your Y-axis intention amplifies, turns up the volume, and brings into focus your relationship with the whole of which you are a part.

Y-axis intentions don't even have to do with healing. If you are ill or out of balance in any way that disturbs the flow of your life, you may feel a strong desire to bring your self back to optimal functioning. Your intention to heal may feel primary, but while we are aligning the Y-axis, this is not the place for that intention. (We will set your healing intentions in the next chapter on the X-axis.) For now, we are opening the main pipeline of life force to flow into your system. Although every cell, organ, and system of your physical body has access to life-force and can communicate directly with Source, it is very beneficial to have the main avenue of the energetic spine flowing life-force into the whole system.

You may have come to this system with a specific need or desire. You may want to heal your body or to find your soul-mate. Maybe you want your art to be appreciated or you want your business to blast off. Whatever motivated you to pick up this book and to stick with it this far must be temporarily put aside right now as we set a more fundamental intention.

Once you align your Y-axis, your other desires refine and redefine themselves. You will become crystal clear about what you want in life and it becomes much easier to achieve your goals. Better than that, you become joyful even when your desires are not fulfilled, and you feel thrilled when they arrive.

You might be surprised if you take an honest look at your life. How many of your past desires that have come into your reality do you thoroughly enjoy? And how many feel like they just brought more problems with them? If you find you are tuned in to the negative aspect of fulfilled desires rather than the joy they bring, this is not a function of the manifestations themselves, it is a function of alignment. You have areas within your energetic spine that are out of alignment and are making it very difficult for your life to have the smooth, enjoyable feel that you want.

By working with this system, you are in the process of doing something about it and you may be amazed at the shift that occurs as you get your Y-axis up and running.

When setting a Y-axis intention before your meditation session, look into yourself and find the purest intention that is real for you at the moment. Pick whatever occurs to you that feels like it has real desire in it. Don't pick what you think you *should* pick. A good Y-axis intention is to feel your love for God and/or God's love for you. Another way to word this type of intention would be to feel your connection to All that is.

You can also set a Y-axis intention to cultivate one of the divine qualities within you. These qualities include unconditional love, compassion, wisdom, kindness, generosity, peace, joy, gratitude. By calling upon one of these qualities, you give your Y-axis intention a specific color and tone that suits you at the moment and that still moves in the direction of the Y-axis. It still opens up your connection with Source energy.

If you find yourself worried, anxious, or depressed, you may be unconsciously trying to hold up your own Y-axis. This feels like you are carrying the weight of the world on your shoulders. You feel you are underneath the downward pressure of the Y-axis and if you let go (emotionally, mentally) your whole world will collapse. You are working so hard and doing such a noble job, but it is too difficult and you feel you are crumbling under the pressure.

There is good news for you. It is not your job to hold up the Y-axis. The Y-axis goes up all by itself. All you need to do is to find your way into the realm of the inner Y-axis. Suddenly, instead of you holding up the Y-axis, it will lift you. You can begin this process by setting a Y-axis intention for faith. Faith brings the feeling that all is well and that all good is available and provided just when it is needed. It softens the air by assuring you that you are safe, that the universe is on your side, that a benevolent force is looking after you, making sure you are taken care of. It allows you to relax and reestablish your connection with your Source. Ahh.

Once you have found an intention that feels right for this session (you can change it every time if you like), feel it, acknowledge it, and then let it go. Your intention setting is done. You won't be thinking about it anymore. The whole thing may take only a few seconds but it sets your course and is of vital importance. Once you have moved through this process, the Y-axis session of the Practice Section is waiting for you.

Y is All You Need

If you came to this system with a purely spiritual intention, then the Y-axis meditation is all you need. Even if you came with varied intentions, the Y-axis is sufficient. Of course we will move on to explore the alignment of the other two axes, but the alignment of the Y-axis is always primary. Next, let's take a look at aligning the X-axis for healing.

See Session Nine of the Practice Section for the experiential
exercises that correspond to this chapter.

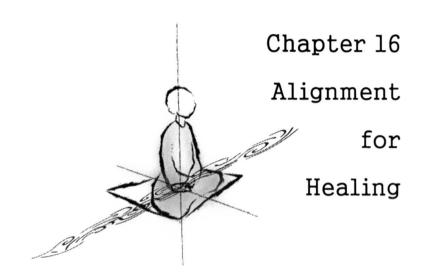

Chapter 16
Alignment
for
Healing

The first thing I'd like to do is phase out this word *healing*. Let's also lighten up on our use of *health*, *heal*, and *healer*. These words all have a wonderful and holy intention. They even trace their ancestry right back to words like *holy* and *whole*. They are excellent words. However, they have gathered multidimensional static around them and they no longer conjure a glowing state of wholeness, joy, and full self-expression. They no longer invoke the sacredness of life.

The opposite more often comes to mind. For instance, the words *health care* reflexively link to the somber tone of *health problems*. When someone tells you to do something for your health, do you immediately expect it to be fun or delicious or even soothing? In fact, it's more likely you think it might be difficult, painful, or require some unpleasant daily discipline. The word *health* is most widely used in the context of disease. It is discussed by people in white jackets. It echoes through the sterile hallways of hospitals. It is rarely whispered in art museums or chanted at rock concerts. No suitor breathes the sweet nothing, "health," into his beloved's ear.

And yet, I have put the word *healing* in the title of this chapter and in the description of the function of the X-axis. I'm using this word because we all know what we mean by it. It acted as a funnel to get you here. Now that we are together, it has done its job. Let's start to be more specific about what we mean. Let's not just grab for these words, using them as code without thinking. They bring a whole trail of vibration with them that may not serve us. As we get more conscious about what we mean when we use words to encapsulate joyful, wholeness of being, this may begin to change. The words *health, heal,* and *healer* may begin to shed some of their conflicting vibration. We may find we can start using them more freely again. I'm not saying we should never use these words. I will continue to sprinkle them in this chapter. I'm simply inviting you to be creative in your use of words around this subject. The subject of health can become highly charged and the more we contribute beneficial word-energies to the subject, the freer we will feel. So, for now, let's just lighten it up a little.

With all that said, let's come up with a word or phrase we can use temporarily to replace the others. Let's feel our way through our rich language and find words better vibrationally suited to what we are looking for when we would otherwise land on the word *healing* or grab the word *health* out of habit.

No matter whether we are talking about a state of body, a state of mind, or something that includes the whole field of being, we want that state to be joyful. Let's be sure to have the word *joyful* in our mix. The wonderful feeling we get when body and mind are finely tuned comes from the smooth interconnectedness of all the parts into a unified and harmonious whole. Let's put the word *harmonious* on our list. Something I learned from Werner Erhard many years ago, and I have found it to be true for myself, is that "health is a function of full self-expression." Lets put "expressiveness" in our recipe.

Okay, here's what we've got so far: health = joyful harmonious expressiveness, or "jhe" for short. (Let's pronounce this jhee.)

Now for the test.

Which of these two expressions is more attractive to you:

"Joyful harmonious expressiveness"

or

"Health"

And which does a more effective job of conjuring the meaning that we are attempting to convey? For me, "jhe" wins. And as I start thinking about getting this energy flowing, this new construct, jhe, acts like a prism tossing rainbows around the room. It shines sunlight on the petals in the garden. It flutters like a butterfly. It is a happy, happy energy.

In the last chapter, we opened ourselves to the natural spring of upward flowing energy of the Y-axis. That's not all we did. We devoted ourselves to a spiritual priority. "Yoga" means to "yoke" oneself to the divine. In our sacred, private moments of spiritual union via the Y-axis, we made our relationship to Source our navigational North Star.

Now, we can look at the flow of jhe as we turn our attention toward taking care of the body/mind aspect of our human instrument.

We will be flowing life force in along the Y-axis and out via the X-axis as our method of attaining jhe. We will follow a similar strategy in the next chapter when we turn our attention to the Z-axis. Both the X and the Z-axes travel in the horizontal dimension. We have spent many chapters together mapping out our vertical journey through the chakras. We've given almost no attention to the horizontal journey. So, before we start moving into our jhe flowing exercises, let's look at the path the energy will follow as it flows outward from the energetic spine.

Working with Your Bodies

Have you ever stood on the shore with your toes in the sand watching the waves as they roll in? You can see the individual waves and follow their pathway, but how would you determine where a wave begins and ends? Maybe you've never been to the ocean, but I'm sure you have felt a breeze. Same question. Where are the boundaries of the wind? These identifiable forms, waves and breezes, have no definite skin around them. They are more intense and recognizable at their center and they become more vague and amorphous at their periphery. Then they blend seamlessly into the sea or the sky or whatever medium they call home.

You and I are like that too. You wouldn't know it though. We have a distinct and physical skin that envelops our little God-given piece of real estate. Yes, we are like little houses in which our spirits dwell. In fact, it is a useful analogy to imagine your body as a house because that leaves you room for a yard. You may not usually think of the back or front yard of your body as your "self" in the same way that you identify with what's inside your skin.

Just like the waves and the wind don't end at a skin, neither do you. Your distinct pattern of energy, recognizable as you, vibrates in the air around you. Some people see this as an aura. Others can feel your energy in an abstract way that doesn't easily translate into our language based on the five senses. Have you ever felt someone looking at you from behind even though you could not see him? This is a sense not easily explained by eyes, ears, nose, mouth, or skin.

This invisible and amorphous field around the body has been catalogued in numerous ways. People of many different disciplines and schools of thought have described and named the subtle bodies within and around the physical body. I will be expanding on the system described by Dr. (Mrs.) Charanjit Ghooi under the inspiration of Sathya Sai Baba. If you are already familiar with a different system, you can use that one.

In our pursuit of jhe, we want all of our subtle bodies to come into alignment with the whole. This added dimension brings a depth and thoroughness to our practice that yields measurable results.

In beginning to think of yourself as a wave, imagining yourself as a wave in the ocean may be too big of a leap. Let's return to the still surface of a pond. Now toss in a pebble. The concentric circles that you see give you a perfect sense of these invisible layers of energy emanating from the intense energy core you call your physical body.

Here are the five bodies we will work with in our process of alignment:

1. The first is your physical body. You know all about that one.

2. Around and through the physical body is your etheric body. It corresponds closely to your physical form. According to this system, it extends about 3 inches beyond the body. You may begin to sense all of these subtle bodies as extending to a broader space as you work more deeply with the meditations presented here. The etheric body can be considered a vital part of the body you are used to. The chakras in the etheric body absorb energy from the sun and supply it to the chakras situated at the core (the ones we've been working with).

3. The astral body interpenetrates the physical and etheric bodies and it extends beyond the etheric body. It is

made of light and can appear like a formless cloud or, with spiritual mastery, can take on the exact form of the physical body.

4. The lower mental body interpenetrates the previous three and extends further.

5. The higher mental body also interpenetrates the others and extends even further. The difference between these two mental planes comes down to a difference in density. The higher mental body is so subtle that it blends you seamlessly into the All.

We won't concern ourselves with the many attributes of these different bodies. You may not know how your liver or your spleen do what they do (you may not even know *what* they do), but you trust that if they do it with jhe, all will be well. We will relate to these subtle bodies with the same understanding.

Inner Shelves

In Chapter 10, we talked about the X-axis as the axis of healing. The X-axis is a resting place and it is always available right *now*. When the human aspect gets heavy, when gravity weighs on your physical presence, the X-axis offers a place to rest. Unlike the horizontal platform offered by the Z-axis, most of which is either gone (past) or not here yet (future), the full expanse of the X-axis is constantly present offering you solace. You can always relax onto it. Release your burden. Drop your backpack. Let go of your briefcase. Surrender your pain. Ease your burden. Find relief. Heal.

We have already talked about the X-axis that lives at your root chakra. There are an infinite number of X-axes that intersect with your Y-axis-energetic-spine and we are about to single out a few more of them which you can work with as you develop your jhe.

Do you have a bookcase in your house? How many shelves does it have? Can you imagine if it were just an outer shell and had no shelves? All the books would be piled, one on top of the other. It would be difficult to manage and not so great to look at. All those bookshelves are little X-axes. They distribute the weight of the books and leave some space around them so you can use them. In other words, the shelves allow the books to perform their function. Without the shelves, your precious tomes would be crushed under their own weight and useless to anyone who would want to get value from them.

You can think of your many inner X-axes as shelves within you. They keep things organized, spacious, and highly functioning. They distribute weight in such a way that all parts feel light. These shelves themselves are weightless.

We are about to single out specific energy "shelves" in your body. They are simply reference points. They are neither exact locations, nor do they correspond to perfectly horizontal structures in the body. Everything is curved and rounded in your anatomy. And yet we do find certain structures that hint at the X-axis and these are the ones we will use in our cultivation of jhe. These X-axis-echoes in the body resonate strongly with the essential nature of the X-axis. As we use them to align ourselves with the X-axis within our consciousness, we experience a soothing, supportive, restful energy. It brings a sense of relief to a challenging situation.

I have chosen nine landmarks on the physical body, which we will use loosely in our alignment for healing. Discovering the inherent structural support of these invisible X-axis shelves, and sensing their innate alignment, does great things for the jhe of the system. Let's look at these nine landmarks from bottom to top.

1. Pelvic floor
2. Sacral base
3. Diaphragm
4. Shoulders

5. Jaw
6. Mouth
7. Base of nose
8. Eyes
9. Eyebrows

As you explore the corresponding alignment exercises in the Practice Section, you may get a sense of the redistribution of your weight onto these weightless X-axis "shelves" and you may feel a shudder go through your body. You may feel yourself in a cloud of light and you may even feel temporarily weightless or a greater lightness than you usually feel. This is all part of the resonance being established between the primordial horizon and your unique incarnation. This especially promotes the "harmony" aspect of our jhe formula as it more generally re-establishes the joyful, easy, interconnected, harmonious relationship between all the different parts of you as a whole. Atom-to-atom, cell-to-cell, tissue-to-tissue, organ-to-organ, body to mind, ego to soul, the relationships are infinite and so is the potential expansion of harmony. Because the X-axis is always *here now*, this is the time to develop your jhe.

There is no thought about the past in the X-axis. There is no concern about the future because of an intuitive knowing that when the future arrives it will be experienced as *now* just like this moment of *now* is. It will be an X-axis just like this one.

Because there is no past or future in the X consciousness, there is a disintegrating of any notion of disease or condition that has been named based on its pattern through time. All that is here is the moment and it simply is what it is and we simply hold it in the grid of our heightened X/Y awareness. Like putting soft, pale, mushy dough in the oven and having it come out golden brown, nurturing, warm, and delicious, we are baking our doughy creation in this mystical X-Y plane, causing a transformation of our unwanted state into one that others might call health or healing. We are calling it joyful harmonious expressiveness.

See Session Ten of the Practice Section for the experiential exercises that correspond to this chapter.

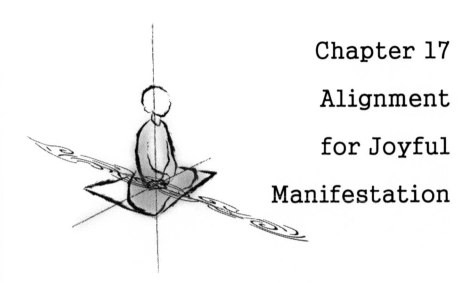

Chapter 17

Alignment

for Joyful

Manifestation

I've learned everything I've needed to know about manifestation from Abraham. From a YOFA™ point of view, manifestation is a Z art. I am so grateful to Jerry and Esther Hicks, the exquisite deliverers of the Abraham message, for shining the headlights of their Z-mobile back and forth across the country, sharing their inner light and transformational teachings. Thanks to the their enormous access to the Y-axis and their generous outpouring of Z energy, ever-increasing numbers of receptive souls are coming to live more joyful, satisfying, and unconditionally loving lives.

Abraham's message teaches us how to come into harmony with life. I have woven this perspective throughout the system offered here as the Yoga of Alignment and I invite you to learn The Science of Deliberate Creation and The Art of Allowing directly from Abraham[1].

The Power of Z

Even though the Z-axis of time rolls out its red carpet eternally, we always stand on its center point of *now*. Manifestation cannot take place in the future because the future never actually occurs.

Manifestation can *only* happen *now*. And so, the first critical point in becoming the artist of your life (and the first blunder to correct if you have been indulging in a belief in the future) is to reel in your attention. Cash in your belief in the future and reinvest your consciousness in this very moment.

The Z-axis of time is real and it is not real. Your forward "facing" face makes time real. Your Y-axis-vertical-spine makes time inconsequential. Your mystical understanding of the point of *now*, the common point in all three of your axes, once developed into wisdom, makes time an art.

The Art of Joyful Manifestation

What do you want? A loving relationship? Material abundance? Success and applause? Sure, you may want these things, but at the core of all these desires is the omni-desire to be happy. How many stories have we heard about the lonely and miserable millionaire or the drug addicted and suicidal superstar? Great accomplishments, the achievement of fame and fortune, all the actual manifestations of desire only fulfill their mission if they also bring heightened access to joy. But if we don't create them that way, in and of themselves, they do not provide lasting joy. That's why so many spiritual paths tell us to run from these desires. They tell us to release them completely.

Abraham offers a completely different understanding of desire, manifestation, and the eternal opening of your experience of *now*. Abraham's revelations about the nature of desire can completely transform our understanding. They reveal the underlying relationship between what has long been thought of as the spiritual path, and what many schools of spirituality would call "worldly." Within the YOFA™ model, it all boils down to the relationship between the Y-axis and the Z-axis. And unless we evolve in such a way that our toes become plumb lines to the earth and our faces sunflowers at noon, we will continue to honor the role of the Z-axis in our human experience.

So, it turns out that the key word in the phrase *Alignment for Joyful Manifestation* is *Joyful*. We are always manifesting. We are always walking into our new manifestation on the mystical treadmill of the Z-axis where each new *now* looks like it was in front of us just a minute ago. Manifesting is automatic. It is only when we bring ourselves to the process in a wakeful and Y-axis-activated state that the creativity becomes deliberate and the manifestation becomes joyful.

It's Personal

Loving relationships, material abundance, overflowing success in your work, fame, fortune, and all the specific desires that bubble within you, these all live on your Z-axis. Your very own Z-axis. They don't live out in the world where they are limited and you have to compete with others in order to get them. They live within your creation as you "move" along your Z-axis.

In Chapter 7, I mentioned that the Z-axis is a personal axis. You can turn it in any direction you like. You can point your nose this way or that way and you won't feel the pull of something like gravity tugging you in any preferred direction. The fact that you can turn anyway you like has an outer and an inner meaning. In the physical realm it means you can move across the earth on your chosen path. In the inner realm it means you have absolute creative freedom.

Creative Freedom

While your face points you in the direction that you are going in the physical realm, it is your focus which formulates the reality in front of you in the inner realm. You then step into your created reality with the feeling that it was always there, waiting for you in the stillness of space. But that understanding superimposes the stillness of the Y-axis perspective (space) on your understanding of time.

This is a very common, unintentional understanding of life. And it would be fine except that it perpetuates a distortion. It disempowers you as a creator. It grabs the paintbrushes from your hands and locks you in a museum as an observer. It makes you think that the reality you are walking into in each moment is already there, frozen in time, just waiting for you. It seems like you have no say in the matter. You have no creative power in that understanding.

If we switch our vantage point and look at the Z-axis from its own perspective, we find a completely different story. In this one, you have tremendous creative freedom. And since either explanation will prove itself as true, depending only on in which one you place your faith, why not try this new one? Then check into your inner garden now and then. See how the flowers are doing. Is the new idea bearing fruit? Is there greater love, joy, and wisdom in your everyday experience?

We already mapped out how the *now* moves (in no-time) up the energetic spine to create your reality. Now we are going to look at how your reality takes form from the perspective of the Z-axis. There are three ways we can look at this and each one offers a pattern of understanding designed to empower you. Each one tells you that your reality is not some stilted landscape that you are wandering into, but a creative medium that you can mold, and within which you can joyfully create the work of art that is your life experience.

The 3 perspectives we are about to explore are:

1. Your reality is the leading edge of your Cascade of Neutralization
2. Your reality results from your interaction with the Universal Law of Attraction
3. The Z-axis is a Wormhole leading to your heart's desire

Cascade of Neutralization

We have already seen how the universe is created anew in each moment of *now*. The Y-axis perspective gave us an understanding of the birthing of each new *now* as an individual big bang. It revealed that since these moments of explosive creation are experienced in uninterrupted sequence, that they create a smooth flow of reality with no perception of explosion.

One big difference between the Y-axis and the Z-axis perspective is that the Z-axis is personal. When you gaze from the Z perspective at these bursts of creation, you can see very clearly how you determine the reality you live. You discover a very personal, intimate connection between you and your unfolding reality.

The light of your attention is like a flashlight. It points in a specific direction. In your inner world, that becomes your inner Z-axis. The field into which you shine your light is filled with something like the tiny charged ping-pong balls we talked about before.

These non-physical little bits of potential manifestation are moving and flitting all around you. They are bouncing and colliding and remaining in their potential state, all looking alike. Once the light of your focus, like a flashlight, shines in a direction, all those points of potentiality that receive your light become highly energized. They begin to collide with such force that they burst into explosions of neutralization as they merge. In that process, they create your reality. The neutralized little sparkles of potentiality fuse into a picture. They became one *now* in the Z orientation. Like one frame in a movie, they produce one infinitesimally small increment of awareness. And it big-bangs itself into your experience. And this happens so close to the one before it and the one after it that you think it is a 3-D still life that is waiting for you to walk into it. Really it is more like a cascade of neutralization and you are on the leading edge of that movement. It is being created at the moment you are living it. It is all happening *now*.

Once you realize that not only is the universe being created in every instant, but it is being created in response to your activation of energy potentiality, now you are on the trail of becoming, as Abraham says, the *deliberate creator of your reality*. You can see that you were always a creator, because your attention was always activating manifestation from the field of charged potential. But as you begin to point your attention with more intentionality, the landscapes you walk into have more people you love and who love you. They have more beautiful scenery and more happy times.

So, how do you know where and how to shine your flashlight so that the bursts of neutralization form into the reality you desire? We will approach this in two ways. First we will talk about what you can do with your conscious awareness to use your attention deliberately. Then, in the Practice Section, you will find meditations you can do for this purpose.

Universal Law of Attraction

The schoolteacher tightly wrapped a copper wire around a great big nail. This coiling of metal and the magnetism it inspired caused all the 10-year-old jaws to drop in amazement. Magnetism is mesmerizing. It wowed us when we were students in that classroom.

You and I are older now. It takes a little more to impress us. What if you attracted into your life a mutually loving relationship with the mate of your dreams? What if you were doing the work and living the life you've wished for since childhood? What if the powerful magnet is not the science project on the teacher's desk, but the magnet is you? And what if you are attracting all the wonderful things, situations, and experiences your heart desires?

Since page one of this book, you have been coiling non-physical energy around your core, your energetic spine. You have been magnetizing yourself. You have been enhancing your relationship with Law of Attraction. It's not that Law of Attraction is now stronger for you than it was before or than it is for others. Law of Attraction is constant. It's just that you are bringing yourself into alignment with the laws of magnetism. The nail can participate with the laws of magnetism by bringing all its parts into alignment. When it does this, it becomes a magnet. Before that, it was only a nail, vulnerable to other magnets. All it did was observe and react. Now, with its magnetism established, it has mastery. Now it attracts "intentionally."

By working with the principles presented in this book and practicing the alignment exercises in the Practice Section, you are coming into alignment in a way that increases your magnetism. You are stepping into the game, increasing your field. You are being the magnet.

The Z-axis Wormhole

We have talked about flashlights and ping-pong balls and magnets, but the question still remains: How do you work with all this to create the reality you desire?

It's pretty simple as long as you understand one essential point. Abraham tells us this over and over and in a very light-hearted way. *You never get it done.*

So if you think that the purpose of all this magnetizing and creating is to get all the stuff you want and then you'll be happy, you are sitting backwards on the horse. The purpose of all this manifestation is for the joy of the process. Of course, that process includes the fulfillment, but the achievement of a goal is only a small segment of the process. And it is not only a small segment but it is a tricky segment.

Have you noticed that, in the garden, the culmination of the plant is the fruit? And yet, within the fruit there are brand new desires in the form of seeds. Once you blossom into a spectacular relationship, or a booming career, or financial abundance, new desires are born within you like seeds in a watermelon. It never ends. So wouldn't it be better to enjoy the whole process?

Now here's the tricky part. Let's say you are willing to wait until your desires are fulfilled before you'll be happy. You are willing to sacrifice your happiness through all the process time. You are willing to work hard and be miserable until the moment when the goodies start pouring in. You're patient and "virtuous" enough to wait for some condition to change before you'll be happy. With this approach, you unintentionally slow down the manifestation.

I'm not sure why we do that, but many of us do. Maybe we think by holding this position of suffering that we will be more deserving of the manifestation. Maybe we believe that it will be more sure to come to us because we have suffered. Whatever the reason, when we do this, once again, we are heading north but facing south. We are moving in the opposite direction of that which we desire. This starts us on a long, arduous journey.

So, please don't be tricked. There is a short cut. It's another wormhole. Just like the one we saw in the Y-axis, it connects two seemingly distant locations by way of an inter-dimensional corridor. Abraham says, "Through the corridor of my joy is the pathway to my desire."[3] That corridor of joy is the wormhole.

The corridor of joy is not the corridor of suffering. It is not the path of being miserable until conditions change. It is not the path of waiting for fulfillment before I'll be happy.

It is the inner path of finding joy and satisfaction and fulfillment right now. That means every *now*, no matter what. This is the path of mastery. It is the way of magnetism. It is the unwavering commitment to feeling good. Feeling good is a reflection of being connected to Source. Being connected to Source is like being connected to the battery if you are a wire-coiled nail. Source is the great magnet that empowers all other magnets.

You can tell you are connected when you feel good. When you feel bad, check your wires. You are losing your magnetism. You are moving in the direction of misalignment rather than greater alignment. This is why it's good to get clear on your Y-axis desires (spiritual intentions) first. They set the tone for the Z-axis manifestations. Then, when you get your car, or your husband, or your big paycheck, these wonderful manifestations bring joy and peace and wisdom in their unfolding.

So this shortcut through the apparent conditions to the fulfillment of your heart's desire is a wormhole, a corridor of joy. As you move through this corridor, you are happy in each stage of unfulfillment of your formulated desire. Not only does this make your life experience more satisfying, it gives you practice at being joyful. If you are not well practiced at joy, then when your desires are fulfilled you may not be equipped to enjoy them.

What are you doing as you move through the wormhole? Well, even the wormhole is not what it seems. Remember the apparent landscape that you thought existed for you to walk into? We found out it was being created by you in every moment of *now*. The same is true for the wormhole. You create the wormhole. You bend time and space through the power of your magnetism. You do this by becoming what Abraham calls "a vibrational match" to that which you desire.

Once you are ringing the same tone as that wonderful relationship you desire, you and the relationship are the same. Law of Attraction must bring you together. If we could put you in an imaginary vibration-reading chamber, and our instruments could read your point of attraction, even though conditions might say otherwise, if the meter tells us that your vibration matches the reality you desire, it must come to you. You match your desire and it arrives at your door. That's how the wormhole works. Abraham has numerous processes for coming into vibrational alignment with your desires. The book *Ask and it is Given*[4] is loaded with them. If you are serious about this, buy that book and read it over and over.

Basically it comes down to keeping your attention on what is wanted rather than the lack of it. The Practice Section at the end of this book is your training ground for what is called concentration or Dharana in yoga. This is the art of holding your mind on one point with such purity and fluidity that it becomes your whole field of awareness. This then becomes what we call meditation. By doing these exercises on the chakras and the axes, you have been developing the exact skill you need to create along the Z-axis.

Pure Thought

Pure thought means unconflicted thought. It means thinking about one thing and one thing only. If you are interested in creating the relationship of your dreams, it means thinking about that relationship so purely that you create the wonderful feeling that you desire from that relationship[5]. It is as if you already have it. If we put you in the imaginary vibration-reading chamber, it would read out that you are in a wonderful relationship. And just as the chamber would read you that way, so does Law of Attraction. And it begins immediately setting the wheels of the world in motion for the manifestation of your vibrational statement.

My favorite of the Abraham processes is the 68 second process. Pure thought for as little as 68 seconds is enough to launch your most cherished desires. Of course, it can take a while before you get 68 seconds of pure thought. But knowing that 68 seconds is all it takes is awe-inspiring. Your creative power is enormous when you consider the number of 68 second increments you have available to you in your lifetime.

The secret of this whole thing, and the reason why you don't have as many of your dreams come true as you would like, rests on one simple factor. Once we have achieved pure thought on the subject of our desire, we tend to go back to contradicting it with our habitual mix of vibration.

Faith

This is where faith in Law of Attraction comes in. When I work with people, I have one major goal in mind and I will hold this for you, too. I would like you to come to trust Law of Attraction the same way that you trust gravity. Right at this moment you are probably not too worried that you will tear right off the earth. You are not concerned that your house will float into the air while you are at work. You trust gravity implicitly.

When you come to know that Law of Attraction is just as reliable, then you begin to place your thoughts with the same care that you place grandma's good dishes. You don't fling them into mid air hoping they'll stay suspended. You place them carefully in the cabinet. You know exactly what gravity will do. It is completely predictable. You work with it to create your desired outcome.

I'd like you to develop this sort of relationship with Law of Attraction, one where you see that it is very predictable and you know exactly what to do to create the desired outcome. All you need to know is that what you are thinking and feeling is being matched by Law of Attraction. What you are thinking and feeling and speaking and focusing upon is what you are getting.

You may say this can't be true. You may think you are intensely focused upon what you want and yet it still hasn't come. If you are focused intensely on something and it has not come, all that means is that you are oscillating between focusing on what you want and noticing the lack of it in your experience. All it takes is a little tweaking toward pure thought for it to come barreling toward you. All it takes is pure thought in a field of faith, confidence, and belief in Law of Attraction, and the thing you desire will be yours.

You have that kind of faith when you order something from a catalog. Once you order it, you wait, trusting that it is on its way to you. That is the sort of relaxed trust and confidence that you can have in Law of Attraction. You launch your desire and you absolutely know it is coming. You eagerly, confidently look for signs of its delivery. You stay awake for inspired action to move you to the fulfillment of this desire (which you know will carry with it the seeds of many new watermelons.)

Baking Bread

Why don't we already trust Law of Attraction? After all, nobody had to teach us about gravity. We learned about it in the course of life experience as babies. Why don't we already know all about Law of Attraction in the same way?

Law of Attraction is more like baking bread. You add all the ingredients, and once it is baked, none of the ingredients are recognizable anymore. You would never know there was an egg in there. You can't see any liquid in it. It's not wet. And yet you know you put some liquid ingredients in there.

All your thoughts, feelings, desires, and resistances are in the bread of your experience. But when you live it, it's one big loaf of bread. You don't see all the ingredients clearly. However, if you start fiddling with the recipe and add more pure thought and leave out some resistance (resistance means focusing on the lack of what you want), you will find that you are baking a whole new kind of bread. You will become an expert baker in no time. This is what we are doing here. We are purifying our vibration for the purpose of making delicious bread.

Here's one last thought on this subject before we move on to the Practice Section. Since desire is so natural, you don't really have to work very hard on this. The more you can relax and trust your inner being to turn your head, the more joyful your Z experience will turn out to be. The Z-axis can be experienced as a wonderful journey. James Taylor said it like this:

"The secret of life is enjoying the passage of time.

Any fool can do it. There ain't nothing to it."[6]

That's it in a nutshell.

See Session Eleven of the Practice Section for the experiential exercises that correspond to this chapter.

Chapter Notes

[1] You can find out all about the teachings of Abraham at the official Abraham-Hicks website at www.abraham-hicks.com or contact Abraham-Hicks Publications, P.O. Box 690070 , San Antonio, TX 78269, Phone: 830-755-2299, Fax: 830-755-4179

[2] For a more in depth exploration of the Art of Joyful Manifestation and the primary role of joy in that process, visit www.VirtualWorkshops.net and listen to the YOFA™ Virtual Workshop called *The Art of Joyful Manifestation.*

[3] Esther and Jerry Hicks, *The Teachings of Abraham: Well-Being Cards* (www.hayhouse.com: Hay House, 2004)

[4] *Ask and it is Given*, by Esther and Jerry Hicks (The Teachings of Abraham) can serve as the Z-axis manual that will map out your journey to whatever you desire. Hay House, 2004.

[5] Find a detailed system for manifesting the romantic relationship of your dreams at the YOFA™ Great Relationships website at www.GreatRelationships.net

[6] Words and Music by James Taylor, *Secret O'Life* (Country Road Music, Inc., 1977)

Chapter 18

A Good Life

We plant a seed and wait. When the seed finally produces the flower we so desired, that flower then produces a new seed. When we follow any desire long enough to witness its full manifestation, it takes us to the starting point of a new desire. This journey, from desire to manifestation to desire, brings either suffering or joy depending on how we approach life. We have begun learning and practicing this YOFA™ method of aligning the ego with the transcendent Self so that, whether we are in the desire portion of the cycle or we are reaping the manifestation, we find joy in the process. We are beginning to value both the process and the manifestation. We see that they are, just like the root and the crown chakras, one and the same.

We've taken a journey together. The inner alignment exercises in the Practice Section bring it all home. They introduce you to your unique X, Y, and Z-axes. Participating with the Practice Section takes this process from an intellectual pursuit to a revelation of Self. From knowledge to wisdom. From mine to yours.

Splitting the Atom of Desire

At many junctions in this exploration we have had to grapple with the stance we are taking on the subject of desire. Our position seems to offer a direct contradiction to traditional yogic philosophy. As usual, the words themselves contribute to the confusion. The idea of *desire*, if we crack it open, can solve the entire puzzle.

I like to talk about the "atom of desire" because, even though by definition an atom is the smallest, most primary substance, we have found that the atom itself is made of smaller components. Similarly, in the past we have thought that desire was the singular component in what we call *desire*. We thought we could relate to it as a singular "substance" that would always behave the way we know desire to behave.

And yet, Abraham has split the atom of desire for us. Abraham has exposed the subatomic nature of what we have been calling desire. With this infor-

mation, we can have a much more successful life experience. We can relate to desire more accurately. We can navigate through its rapids with skill and confidence.

The funny thing is that the revelation has more to do with words than anything

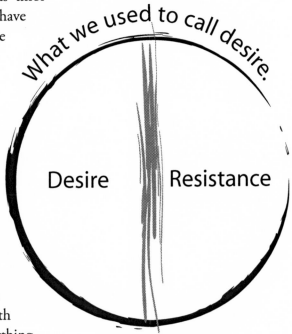

What we used to call desire.

Desire   Resistance

else. And yet, by speaking more accurately abut this volatile subject, we transform our entire relationship with desire. It's very simple, and yet, like splitting the atom, the energy released can completely transform your life. (In this case, for the better.)

What we have been calling desire is like a big cloud of energy that includes the actual desire along with the resistance to the desire. In the new language we are developing through the clarity of Abraham's message, we will call only the desire *desire*. We will call the resistance *resistance*. Once we do this, we find that the spiritual teachings have always been condemning the resistance portion of the desire. Since we were not distinguishing the resistance from the desire, and since we were calling the whole thing *desire*, the whole thing got condemned.

Now, as we recognize that the desire is the *yes*, it is the pure flow of energy, it is the life force, it is the continuity of God flowing though the human instrument, we find nothing in it to condemn. As we see that the resistance is the *no*, the doubt, the separation from Source, the stance of "ego," the obstruction to the flow of Divine Energy, we see that it is our resistance, not our desire, that we want to dissolve. And once we see that resisting *resistance* is about as useless as desiring *desirelessness*, we are left with only one simple path to take to our most cherished goal. We must desire purely. Whether our desires flow along the Y-axis, the X-axis, or the Z-axis, by focusing purely and joyfully on our desire, we naturally and automatically release resistance. In this way, we find the path of desire and the path of desirelessness are the same path. It becomes crystal clear once we realize that the more accurate translation of *desirelessness* is *resistancelessness*.

Now we are all seeking the same thing. Now we can proceed in our spiritual practice, in our business, in our relationships, and in our healing with one single strategy. We have one universal approach to life that works on all fronts.

The Secret of Now

It is time to understand the living meaning of *now*.

Now is Self.

Since now is eternal,

Self is immortal

Self is synonymous with *being*. This same infinity that is *now*, *here*, and *being* (Z, Y, and X), when held wholly (holy) in its multi-dimensional glory, when beheld in its dynamic, incomprehensible evolution, is Self.

As you look into your current situation, your job, your home, your relationships, your body, your world, see that this *now* moment is the face of the Self. The more deeply you look into the eyes of the *now*, the more clearly you see your Self. They are one and the same.

The inner garden that we have been tending turns out to be the garden of the Self and it exists only at that extraordinary point where *here*, *now*, and *being* intersect. We water this garden by pouring our uninterrupted pure consciousness on its fertile ground. We cultivate with the practices of concentration and meditation, which weed out conflicts in our vibration and bring forward the sweet fruit of our hearts' desires.

Now that you understand this system of alignment, you can easily put it into practice. The Practice Section guides you through a series of meditation/concentration processes designed to assist you in training yourself into alignment. As you work with these, you will find that some areas call for greater attention than others. Follow your inner guidance to get the greatest value.

If you already have a meditation practice, the Yoga of Alignment meditations may serve as a bridge to lead you more smoothly into your regular practice. When practiced before other types of sitting meditation, they ease the transition from the busyness of the day-to-day consciousness to the meditative state of inner peace.

Thank you for joining me on this journey.

See Session Twelve of the Practice Section for the experiential exercises that correspond to this chapter.

Miscellaneous Notes

Back Cover: Fortune from *Golden Bowl Fortune Cookies*
Page 63: What do you think this picture is? Check the website www.RootedintheInfinite.com

Practice Section

Introduction

YOFA™ Training cultivates access to the Infinite. In this system, you train your finite instrument into energetic alignment with your inner nature so that it becomes free from obstructions. The breath of pure beingness can then blow through the shape of your individual consciousness to produce the beautiful music of your life.

When we think of training, we tend to think of discipline. And when we think of discipline, we may be excited about the call to excellence while cringing at the anticipation of pain. We know we will have to do something that we don't want to do when we don't want to do it. Or, we will have to refrain from doing what we want to do when we want to do it. That is the requirement of discipline: resisting our natural tendencies for a greater purpose.

YOFA™ Training is completely different. And yet it does ask a paradoxical discipline of you. It asks you to do what you want to do when you want to do it. This is only a discipline in the sense that you have been so trained away from your inner guidance, that finding it, and re-sensitizing yourself to it, and re-establishing your trust in it requires a little work on your part. But it is work that might better be called play since you know you are doing it "right" when it feels good.

As you move through the Practice Section, do only the exercises that call to you. Do them only when you want to do them. Do them for as long as they feel engaging to you. Basically, you are training yourself into tune with your desire.

There is one more thing to consider here. That is Law of Attraction. Since this universal system of magnetism has been responding to your habitual imprint of misalignment, as you begin to make efforts toward alignment you will feel like you are going against the flow. And you will be. You will be moving your attention in the direction opposite to the flow of *conditions*. It helps to reset your sites to the flow of *well-being*. Once you recalibrate by seeking your resonance with well being at all times, you will find it much easier to move with your new intention. This is where Abraham suggests we take the stance that, "nothing is more important than that I feel good."

As you experiment, play, explore, and more deeply meet yourself in this way, you train yourself into mastery.

I've organized this so that you can go through this section after you've read the book or you can read the book and explore each chapter's alignment exercises as you go.

As a training in alignment, it would be of advantage to spend a week to a month on each session before moving on to the next. However, you may want to explore each session as you read the book, then return to the first session to begin your training.

Some sessions have several alignment exercises. You may want to divide these sessions and do one exercise per day.

Before each alignment session, please review the pre-meditation checklist in Chapter 4. Audio versions of these exercises are available at www.RootedintheInfinite.com.

*This practice session
corresponds to chapter*

6

Your eyes will be closed much of the time as you venture inward to find your root. This is a highly personal process and no one can tell you if you are doing it right. If you are taking the time to look within with a clear mind and an open heart, you are doing it "right" and good will come of it.

As you close your eyes and begin to look for the area of the root chakra in your experience, it will help to have a map. Together we can construct the map we need by looking at an imaginary piece of energy-sensitive film that shows the energy imprint of the chakra. The meditator in the illustration will be our model. Let's suppose that he is sitting in a modified lotus posture on an energy-sensitive film. Upon rising, he leaves a distinct pattern on the film.

Here's a diagram of the energetic imprint of the root chakra with its anatomical landmarks.

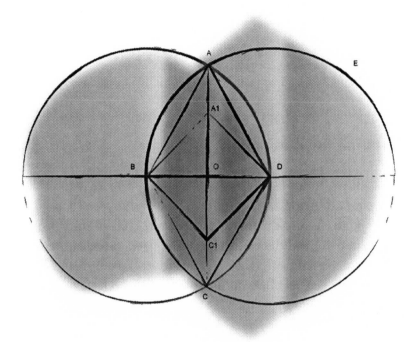

Locating the Outer Casing

First we see the circular energy imprints of his buttocks, which we will call the outer casing of the chakra (E). Our first inquiry into the experience of the root chakra will be to sense the outer casing of the chakra formed by the buttock circles.

Outer Casing Exercise

Close your eyes and feel your weight evenly distributed on both buttocks. Sense the shape of the base upon which you rest. Spend a couple of minutes allowing your awareness to settle on this foundation created by the buttock circles.

Locating the Z-axis

Looking more closely at the film, we begin to see the front and back landmarks of the chakra. These points correspond to the pubic bone (A) and the root of the genitals (A1) in the front, and the coccyx (C) and the anus (C1) in the back. (see diagram) If we connect these points by drawing a line that extends through them and beyond the body, we outline the Z-axis or forward-backward direction of the root chakra. Our next exploration into sensing the root chakra will take us to the Z-axis as it passes through the center point (O) of the chakra.

Z-axis Exercise

Close your eyes and feel the line of direction that extends infinitely in front and in back of the center point of your root chakra. Let this process help you begin to identify the chakra and its center point. Don't be concerned if it still feels vague. Release all other thoughts and feelings and hold your awareness gently on the Z-axis of the root chakra. Stay there for a few minutes.

Locating the X-axis

The prominent bones within the buttocks are called the ischeal tuberosities but we more commonly refer to them as the *sitting bones*. These bony landmarks establish the side boundaries of the chakra (B and D). When we connect these two points, we outline the X-axis, or the side-to-side direction, of the root chakra. Next, we will locate the X-axis of the root chakra in our inner awareness.

X-Axis

B D

(Pelvis in illustration by Leonardo Da Vinci)

X-axis Exercise

Close your eyes and feel your weight balancing on your sitting bones. Imagine a line connecting the two bones and extending infinitely to the right and the left. This line also passes through the center point of the chakra. Engage your attention on the X-axis of the root chakra for a few minutes as you release all other thoughts.

Locating the Y-axis

Where the X-axis and the Z-axis cross, we find the center of the chakra (O). The vertical Y-axis passes through this same point in the up-down direction. Now let's locate the Y-axis experientially.

Y-axis Exercise

Close your eyes and sense the line that moves right through the center of your body. This is the line that we are calling the energetic spine. It rises directly up from the center point of the root chakra, through the center of your body, and infinitely above you. It also extends below you through the center of the earth and beyond. Feel your posture shift as you become aware of the Y-axis. Feel your body naturally seek to align itself with your inner sense of the vertical axis. Stay with the Y-axis for a few minutes.

Combining All Landmarks

The center point, where the X, Y, and Z-axes meet (O), is the focal point of the chakra. The square we see when we connect the dots of our landmarks (A,B,C,D) illustrates the whole region of the chakra. The square, the hallmark of stability and balance, serves as the shape of the root chakra and outlines the four petaled lotus, the classic symbol of Muladhara. To complete the process of locating the root chakra in our awareness, we will combine all the landmarks on the map and become fully familiar with the inner landscape of the root chakra.

All Landmarks Exercise

Close your eyes and sense the outer casing of the chakra created by the buttock circles. Sense the shape, security, and stability provided by the foundation of the buttocks. Appreciate the safe environment offered by the outer casing for the inner sanctuary of the chakra. Next, sense the Z-axis as a string of light extending infinitely in front of you and in back of you, passing through the center point of the chakra. Once you have a strong sense of the Z-axis, imagine the infinite X-axis string of light passing through the same mysterious point at the center of the chakra and extending infinitely to the right and to the left. Feel the perfection of these strings of light as they begin to align you with your own center. Appreciate the sense of stability and ease that accompanies the discovery of your inner axes. Now sense the Y-axis as it passes through your energetic spine and moves through the same central point shared by the other two axes. Feel your spine shift to align itself with your energetic spine. Feel your three inner axes harmonizing with the three dimensions of the physical universe. Allow a sense of inner peace to enter your awareness. Release all other thoughts as they come into your mind and spend a few minutes enjoying the spaciousness of the three axes as they live inside of you.

ℰ‍ↄ This completes the first session. ℰ‍ↄ

This practice session corresponds to chapter

7

Practice Section

Session 2

Locating

The Now

We are about to close our eyes to align ourselves with the Z-axis of time. To get the maximum benefit from the following exercises, review the pre-meditation checklist before beginning. Then spend some time (how much time is up to you) focusing your attention on the center point of the root chakra. Let all other thoughts and sensations fade as you simply become interested in this small point at the center of time.

Once you have pulled your awareness into this single point, in this set of exercises you will expand your focus to include the forward and backward limbs of the Z-axis. Sometimes, in the practice of concentration, it is useful to give the mind a variety of things to focus on to keep it from wandering. Like the buttons, bells, and beads on the baby's busy box, this type of meditation gives the mind a lot to play with. While providing the mind with beneficial content, it transparently reels in the mind, circling it in closer and closer to the focal point of the chakra.

Z-axis Meditation on the Past

As you sit on the infinite expanse of your forward flowing Z-axis, bring your attention to its back limb, the past. Recognize that while you look back at the past, the point you look from is always the center point of the now. What you experience as the past is simply a dimension of now. As we turn our attention to the past, let's set an intention to heal, harmonize, and spread love as we go. Let's transform our memory of the past into a soft cushion which comfortably supports us as we move forward.

Knowing that what appears to be the past is contained in the now, hold the infinite stretch of Z behind you in your loving awareness. As it recedes into the fog of time and distance, realize that you cannot understand all the infinite causes that led you to the point at which you now stand. Know that in this moment, the most powerful gift you can give to your past is love. And that love will transform both your present moment and your past memories.

As you breathe in, imagine the breath entering your energetic body from the root chakra. Let the breath collect in the area of the chakra and there imagine it transforming into love. As you breathe out, send this love backward through the channel of your root chakra's Z-axis. Imagine a smooth flow of soothing love pouring from your present self, like a stream, filling every nook and cranny of your past. It may help to imagine the backward flowing limb of the Z-axis as a plant's root that branches to all your past experiences.

First let the love fill the part of the root nearest to you. Let it soothe your most recent moments of hurt, fear, anger, violence, or perhaps disappointment or loss. Allow any specific memories that come to mind to find their place in the root and be transformed by the love flowing to and through them. You are not condoning anything that you deem to be bad in the past. You are simply loving the whole of your experience. You are loving the one who had the experience.

Once your most recent past feels calm and serene, flow your love further back. Send the love through each different episode of your life in as much or as little detail as comes naturally to you. If memories present themselves easily, without judging their significance or their tone, simply allow the love to flow to that branch of the root. If no memories surface, let an abstract sense of love flow behind you filling every point on your already-lived timeline.

When you get to your birth, keep going back to the womb. Send love back to your nonphysical self before you were born. Keep letting the love flow to your previous incarnations. Like pearls on a string, see your unknown lifetimes and fill them with love.

Let the love ease the pains both remembered and forgotten. Let the love flow so far back in time that you cannot even imagine its destination. With your love comes an honoring of all your past decisions, a forgiving of what you see as past mistakes, and a gratitude for the journey that brought you here. Feel a softening of the pain of the past. Feel the jagged edges of *the memories that have made you cringe begin to shape themselves into harmonious waves.*

Honor your past feelings by opening to the possibility that you have learned all you needed to learn from that pain. Sense that the suffering served a purpose and that, like a jewel that has been through an uncompromising process of purification, you are now enhanced, enlightened, and enlivened by all that your soul has experienced thus far.

Hold gently any experience of vulnerability that you have felt in the past. Like wrapping a baby in a blanket, swaddle your past tenderly with compassion. See your past trials as labor pains birthing your consciousness into the eternal now.

See the line of light extending infinitely behind you. Sense the ancient continuity of your soul. Give thanks for your existence. Follow the line forward to the present moment, the center point of your root chakra. Feel the power of your now.

Z-axis Meditation on the Future

Close your eyes and imagine that you are seated at the fulcrum of the seesaw of future and past, facing the future. Feel the two ends of the seesaw teeter-totter until they come to a point of balance. Look out ahead of you at the infinite line of Z. Shine a light and see how far it illuminates. Then move your mind to the limits of that light and shine another. Again

move to the limits of that light and shine another. Do this several times until you have the sense of an enormous abundance
of time extending great distances in front of you. As you do
this, stay aware of the now point where you sit. Feel the power
of the now from where you navigate.

*As you breathe in through the root chakra, feel the breath
pool and transform into a mixture of love, joy, and wisdom.
Let it collect for several breaths until you feel a small reservoir
of love, joy, and wisdom filling the foundation of your energetic
body. Breathe energy right in through the center of your root
chakra. Once you feel it's soothing presence glowing in the lowest part of your torso, begin the next step.*

*As you exhale, glide this energy mixture out in front of
you. First let it fill the space right in front of you. Then, with
each out breath let it move further and further. Let it cross the
room until it reaches the wall opposite where you sit.*

*As you exhale again, it still flows forward on its own mo-
mentum and gets a thrust forward with each exhalation. With
the next exhalation of this love-joy-wisdom-breath, let it flow
right through the wall and beyond the edge of your house or
building. See it continue on and on to your entire neighbor-
hood and beyond. Let it travel out into the infinite expanse of
space. Know that as you pave the way of your future with a
sacred vibration that resonates with your inner truth and your
heart's true desire, you will be able to step into each new now
guided by wisdom, lifted by joy, and filled with love.*

Z-axis Meditation on the *Now*

> As you sense the infinite forward and backward expanse of the Z-axis, recognize its center as the center point of the root chakra at the perineum. Feel the simultaneity of past, present, and future in the now. With this awareness, release your attention from the extremities of the axis and bring your focus home to the region of the center of the chakra. As your awareness gathers itself to a singular point, experience your breath as it moves in and out through the center point of the chakra. Feel the sufficiency of this point. Feel the creative power of this point. Then just feel the point. The point and the breath. As your mind wanders, gently bring it back. Concentrate your mind. Release all else. This point creates your reality as you know it. By bringing your uninterrupted awareness to this point, you gain access to the presence of the now. This is where you are rooted in the Infinite.

Z-axis Meditation on Flow

> Imagine you are sitting on a four-petalled lotus floating on a stream. The current carries you at a comfortable pace and you are surrounded by color, beauty, and the sweet sounds of nature. Feel the gentle breeze against your face as you move perpetually forward. The view is continually interesting, ever changing and engaging. You can speed up or slow down as you desire. Feel the Z-axis movement that is your relationship with time.

Recommended Z-axis Meditation Session

1. Review pre-meditation checklist (Chapter 4)
2. Locate root chakra in meditation using exercises in Session 1
3. Z-axis meditation on the past
4. Z-axis meditation on the future
5. Z-axis meditation on the now
6. Flowing with the Z-axis

ℰ This completes the second session. ℰ

This practice session corresponds to chapter

8

Practice Section

Session 3

Locating

The Center of

the Universe

B efore beginning the Y-axis root chakra meditation session, I recommend reviewing the pre-meditation checklist. You can further prepare yourself by doing all the meditations already described, even if you just touch on them briefly. Locating the chakra as described in Session 1, and aligning the Z-axis as described in Session 2, will optimize your experience as we enter the vertical dimension.

Aligning with Gravity

The relationship between the earth and gravity sets up the Y-axis. Because of the earth and it's gravitational force, up and down are not equivalent for us. With earth as the element of the first chakra, and foundation as its meaning, we can see how the root chakra's job is to hold us up in the face of the force that would otherwise pull us down. It does this job through the mysterious vertical up-force.

This up-force, accessible through meditation on the root chakra, rises so powerfully that is said to bestow the supernatural power of levitation upon its practitioner. You probably don't need to pad your ceiling just yet. You may not physically lift off the ground, but the more important upliftment, the inner lightness of spiritual awareness, will surely rise with your concentration on the vertical component of the root chakra. If you do lift off the ground, don't say I didn't warn you.

Aligning the Base

Close your eyes and visualize the chakra. See the four cardinal points creating a square with its corners at the front, back, and sides. Now see a peg running vertically through the center point of the chakra. Connecting the dots creates two pyramids with their bases touching. Check all the angles between the axes to make sure they are square. Sense the stability offered by this structure. Then feel the vertical axis as it extends upward through the spine. Allow your posture to shift and adjust to accommodate your heightened sense of the vertical. Imagine a point at the center of the top of your head where the vertical passes through as it continues on above you through the infinite expanse of space. Imagine it also extending infinitely below you. Then return your attention to the vertical column within the center of the double pyramid. Hold your attention there for a few minutes. When you're ready, open your eyes.

Breathing Through the Doorway

Close your eyes and find the vertical dimension of the root chakra. Allow this channel to be the pathway of your breath. As you breathe in, feel the breath rise from the undifferentiated universe just below your root chakra. Let it flow into your body, filling the region of the chakra. As you breathe out feel it exit the chakra through the same pathway. The friction of the breath may bring the egg into focus. If you feel the egg, you can let your mind use it as a focal point for your concentration if you like. It doesn't matter at all if you do not feel it. Simply continue to sense your breath as it flows easily through the doorway of the chakra. If your mind is active, say Om out loud on each out breath until you sense yourself quieting down. Then say it silently. Feel the contrast between the stillness of the chakra and the movement of the breath. When you're ready, open your eyes.

ↄ This completes the third session. ↄ

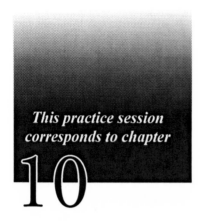

Practice Section

Session 4

Balance and

Healing

This practice session corresponds to chapter

10

The following exercises help you bring the X-axis of your root chakra into alignment. They also help you access the third infinity of this chakra, the inner infinity of being. If you are looking to this system for the purpose of healing, these exercises can support your body, mind, and soul in manifesting the healing that you seek.

Step 1: General Preparation

To maximize your benefit from these exercises, use the tools offered in Chapter 4 to prepare yourself. Follow the instructions for sitting, breathing, intention, and concentration, and use the pre-meditation checklist to give yourself maximum advantage in this process.

Step 2: Specific Preparation

Once you have brought your attention inward, focus your mind on the center point of the root chakra. Feel your breath pass through this point as it enters your body. Then ex-hale down and out through the same point.

Next, feel your sitting bones. Feel your weight evenly distributed on these two bones. If you cannot feel this, imagine it. Feel or imagine the line connecting these two bones (See il-lustration in Practice Session 1, Locating the X-axis). Imagine the point at the center of this line. This point is also the center point of the chakra. Then sense this line extending infinitely in both directions. You are sitting right on the horizon. The broad expanse of the horizontal offers you stability, balance, rest. Take as long as you need to experience the X-axis of the root chakra. Feel this side-to-side axis of the perineum present in your awareness before moving on to Step 3.

Step 3: X-axis Root Chakra Exercises

Exercise 1: Gushing

> *While keeping your attention on the center point of the chakra, expand your awareness to include the buttocks. Feel the large, stable base provided by the buttocks. Then get a sense of the smaller, horizontal band or tube connecting the two buttock circles. This tube passes through the center point of the chakra. Begin to get a sense of this whole structure as a sort of hourglass turned on its side. Each buttock feels like a large bulbous space that opens into the other via a small tube between them.*

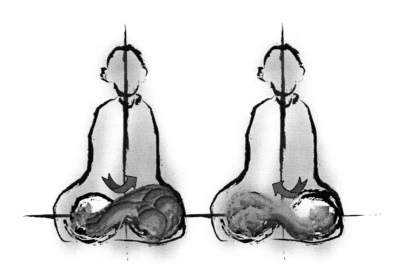

Begin to imagine some energy moving through that small canal, from one buttock to the other. It may help to visualize this energy as water. As it flows back and forth, it fills one buttock and empties out of the other. Then that one empties to fill the first. As you sense this fluid energy pouring through the center point of the perineum, it picks up momentum and becomes a rhythmic wave moving back and forth within the "hourglass" of your foundation. As the flow becomes stronger, like ocean waves, they crash on the sides of the buttock circles as they pour into each buttock, then powerfully flow back out to splash against the wall of the opposite buttock. Feel the majestic and awesome power, like the ocean meeting the shore, with every filling of each buttock.

As the water gushes through the center point, imagine it washing, cleansing, purifying, rejuvenating, and revitalizing the X-axis of the root chakra. When you are ready, bring your attention back to the center point of the chakra, the earth point below the ocean waves of energy.

Exercise 2: Figure 8

With your mind still holding the form of the "extended root chakra" including the buttocks, replace the image of the hourglass with the sideways figure 8, or the infinity sign. Imagine this infinity sign like the figure 8 track of a child's toy train set. The center point of the infinity sign marks the center of the chakra, and the loops trace the path the energy takes as it flows around each of the buttocks.

Imagine a dot of light or a trail of lights following this path through your extended root chakra. Like a toy train, the energy follows the track, touching the center every time around. The light, the train, or whatever image you choose for the energy, will move in from the back and flow out to the front. Watch, feel, or imagine it as it circulates through the region. Let it go at whatever pace feels comfortable. Encourage it to find a smooth and balanced rhythm.

Once it is flowing comfortably, refocus your attention on the center point of the chakra and feel the pulsing or tapping of the energy each time it passes through the center. Let your mind do whatever it has to do to hold both the movement of the energy and the stillness of the center point at the same time. Your mind may go back and forth between visualizing the whole infinity sign to just feeling the rhythm of the tapping at the center. Accept whatever feels the most natural.

Exercise 3: Walking

You can do this as a focused walking meditation or simply play it as a game when you are walking around in your life. With each step you take, feel the energy pour from one buttock to the other. Feel it alternately filling each buttock as it passes through the center point of the chakra. You can help bring awareness to the process by mildly contracting the muscles of the buttock of the leg that is bearing the weight. Which side fills? The buttock of the leg supporting the weight or of the swinging leg? Try imagining both.

෩ This completes the fourth session. ෩

This practice session corresponds to chapter

11

Opening

C lose your eyes and mentally go through the pre-meditation checklist (Chapter 4). Allow your attention to
gently settle on the root chakra. Sense the Y-axis as it
establishes the vertical dimension in your root chakra. Envision it along the energetic spine, adjusting your posture to meet
the vertical as you go. Imagine the Y-axis as a line of blue light,
glowing within you, extending infinitely above you and below
you.

Next, bring your attention to the Z-axis as it extends in
front of you and behind you, far beyond what your mind can
imagine. See this line as red light.

Next, bring your attention to the X-axis as it passes through the center of the chakra. Imagine it as a yellow line extending infinitely to the right and left, balancing and stabilizing you mentally and physically.

At the center point of the chakra, where all three lines touch, find an area of radiant white light, silently glowing. Sense that light as the opening through which the now enters, unfettered, uncolored. Let your mind enter the peace of this region. You rest in the silence of this light. Free from the pull of any external forces, devoid of influence, you are free in the opening of the new moment.

ε∩ This completes the fifth session. ε∩

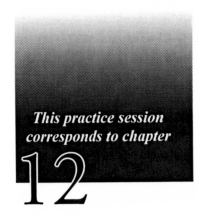

This practice session corresponds to chapter

12

Reviewing the pre-meditation checklist in Chapter 4 is always a good idea before beginning.

Breathe in through the root chakra and let the breath rise to the area just above the root, the region of the second chakra. As you exhale, fill the entire area of the second chakra with vitalizing energy. Do this several times until you feel the area between the sacrum and the pubic bone fill with vitality and awareness.

Next, breathe in through the root chakra and allow the breath to rise to the third chakra at the level of the navel. Exhale filling the entire region of the third chakra with life force as you did with the second chakra. Allow your posture to shift into alignment with the vertical axis created by the alignment of the bottom three chakras.

Fire

See a blazing sun at the center of your belly between the crest of the lumbar spine wave and the navel. Maintaining this highly energized blaze requires no effort from you. Like the sun, it is there to serve you, to warm you, to light your way. The more you open to its gift, the brighter it shines in you. Its flame lets you transform all that comes into your system into beneficial, nutritious energy. It purifies you. It heals you. It empowers you. It motivates you. It energizes you. It propels you forward.

Feel its warmth radiating to every part of your body. See its light illuminating every cell within your physical body. See your body glow with vitality and strength. Imagine your glow extending far beyond the limits of your physical body. Trust the fire burning brightly within you to light your way.

Focus your attention on the third chakra. Silently repeat om as you breathe in and out through the chakra.

Water

Place your attention on the second chakra and sense the nature of the water element. Feel the water nature of your whole body. Feel the soft, fluid, yielding presence of the water vibration throughout your being. Feel all tensions in your body spontaneously release as the notion of water flows through your consciousness. Visualize the fluidity with which the blood flows through your vessels. Sense the continuous, reliable flow of fluids through your physical body. Allow the current of vitality to flow through your energy body. Imagine the steady stream of nows coursing through your energetic spine.

As you breathe, feel the softness of the turning points between inhalation and exhalation. Like gentle waves on the shore, feel the fluidity of your breath. Let your awareness of water's energetic presence remove all the jagged edges from your experience. Let it melt all your hardened patterns of thought. Let it soften your body's inflexibilities. Let it soothe you. Like returning to the womb, let it mother you.

Feeling safe and relaxed, silently repeat om with each breath as you settle your attention on the second chakra.

౪ This completes the sixth session. ౪

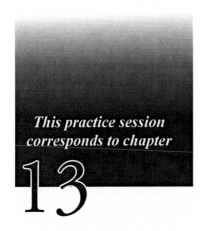

The Stages of Sound

Focus your attention on the root chakra. With each inhalation, imagine the primordial hum of the universe entering your energetic spine through this portal. Once you sense a vibrating, humming fullness in this area, feel it rise to the third chakra at the navel. Sense it taking on shape or color. Sense some abstract meaning within it at this stage of seed thought. Once you feel it filling this region, feel the joy as it fills the garden of the heart. You may swell with feeling at this stage. When it feels natural, let it emerge as voice. You can simply open your mouth and sustain the simple sound "ahh." You can also play with the possibility of words surfacing. See what your heart has to say today.

The Speaking-Hearing Cycle

One you have cleared the pathway from the root to the spoken voice, focus your attention on the heart chakra. Imagine a beautiful flower facing outward and upward from the center of your chest. Practice some relaxed breathing as you allow this flower to become even more beautiful, its colors even more luminous. With your attention still engaged with the flower of your heart, make a sound. Ah, Om, yam, or ham are good choices for this exercise. As soon as you hear the sound with your ears, feel it re-entering your heart and vitalizing the flower. Experiment with sounds and pitches. Find the sounds you can make that resonate with the energy of your heart. Don't worry about sounding funny. If you feel embarrassed, do this where no one can hear you. Spend some time immersed in this cycle. Enjoy the amplification of the heart's vibration as it recurs through your system

Listening With Your Heart

The next time you find yourself in a conversation with someone you love, imagine the flower of your heart. As you listen, feel your loved one's voice being received by the funnel shape of the flower. Feel his or her voice as you would the gentle touch of a hand.

Speaking From the Heart

> *In the same conversation, when you feel moved to speak, let the word selection be guided unconsciously by the preferences of the heart. How do you do this? Set the intention and it will do it all by itself. Open your mouth and let it flow. You will be able to tell instantly, as it re-enters your system, how successful you were.*

Meditation on the Heart

The following meditation comes from the teachings of Master Hilarion, brought forth through Hilda Charlton in the book *The Golden Quest.*

> *Meditate on the heart, the fourth chakra, as a great White Light sending forth rays of Divine Love to the world, blessing all. Do this continually, drawing in the vibration of Love with the will on the inward breath and releasing Love with intense will on exhalation. You will find the heart chakra feeling free and the body relaxed as this is practiced. Make a practice of this during the day as much as possible. Use everyday problems and situations as part of the meditation. Bless everyone you meet, and continually feel the outflow of Love to all alike, free from attachment.*

&c3; This completes the seventh session. &c3;

Practice Section

Session 8

Wisdom &

Mastery

After completing the pre-meditation checklist, focus your attention on the inner point of the funnel of the top two chakras. This point is the root of both the 6ᵗʰ and 7th chakras and both will receive beneficial resonance from your meditation here.

Bring your attention directly forward to the point between and just above the two eyebrows. Imagine your two physical eyes relaxing as you look out through this third eye of wisdom. Look into the darkness, the distance, the unknown through this energy center. Repeat Om on each exhalation.

Here are some formulas for meditation on the transcendent Self borrowed from Swami Sivananda.[1] Use them once you have gone through the pre-meditation checklist and have aligned yourself with the X, Y, and Z-axis. Let your attention settle on your breathing, letting it do whatever it does naturally. Then bring into your awareness one of these phrases. Let it float in the space of your awareness. Let in melt in your mind. Let it dissolve and permeate all reaches of your awareness.

> I am life eternal.
> I am That I am.
> I am absolute consciousness.
> I am all joy.
> I am Infinity, Eternity, Immortality.
> I am present everywhere.
> I am one, complete, whole, perfect.
> I am wisdom, existence, bliss.
> I am the Infinite.
> I am the center.
> I am the foundation.
> I am one with the universe.
> I am one with every being.
> I am one with friend and foe.

There is another time-honored way to approach this shift in identification from the individual self to the transcendent Self within your meditation. You can bring in the question, "Who am I?" Any answers that arise are to be released as incomplete, untrue, or illusory. As they come in, one by one, auditioning for the role of Self, keep letting them go. Do not compromise. We have left the playing field of knowledge and are entering the living land of wisdom. Here, the answer will come not through the mind and its imaginings. Instead it will offer its presence as an intuitive awareness.

We are told that this Self we seek is not something that can be perceived by the senses. Therefore, if your mind answers with something that can be perceived it must be immediately dismissed. The Self cannot be known by the mind because the Self is the knower. If the mind offers an answer to your question that can be known, that is not it either. The Self has no form. It cracks all vessels that would try to contain it. Therefore, if your mind answers with a form, that cannot be it.

This practice is called neti neti or "not this, not this." It is a systematic way of negating all limiting beliefs that perpetuate the pain caused by our small self reality. Ultimately, this practice is said to awaken transcendental consciousness. This path is not for everyone and it is not one of the easier ways to follow. However, if this feels like home to you, you might want to look further into the path of Jnana Yoga or Vedanta.

ဆ This completes the eighth session. ဆ

Chapter Notes

[1] Find these and more Vedantic formulas for meditation here: Swami Sivananda, *Dhyana Yoga* (India: The Divine Life Society, 1994) pages 101-113

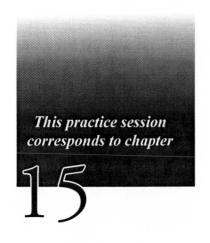

Practice Section

Session 9

Alignment

for Spiritual

Awareness

Breathing into Alignment

O nce you have turned your attention to your natural breath for a few cycles (see pre-meditation checklist), begin sensing your in-breath entering your body through the root chakra. Imagine the infinite, undifferentiated source of life force pouring into your system at your root chakra and filling it with vital energy. As you exhale see the energy expand in all directions in the region of your root chakra. Feel it fill and cleanse that region of your body. Imagine it lighting up the bottom of your energetic spine. Take as many breaths as you need to fill this region with vital energy. It may take only one breath, it may take many.

The feeling reminds me of blowing up a balloon. Once you start to feel some resistive pressure as you exhale into this area, you will know it is filling up. Have you ever tried to blow up an inflatable raft or to fill some other large area with your breath? In the beginning it feels like your air is just a drop in the bucket. It comes out of you and seems to dissipate. It seems to do nothing toward your goal of filling the raft. But if you are persistent, eventually you feel the pressure start to build and you begin to feel the raft filling. Sometimes filling a chakra with life force feels like that. I exhale and it seems to go nowhere. But usually after three or four breaths I can feel the area filling up. I had not noticed this energy deficiency in my outer directed, daily awareness. But the more I look inward, the more I can balance these deficiencies before they become un-comfortably noticeable. So, don't worry if you find some difficult chakras to fill. You can be very happy that you are now taking the time to enjoy filling them. The "fullness" of your chakras may vary greatly from session to session. Without making any value judg-ments about the process, simply become interested in the feeling of filling your lower torso with aliveness.

Please note that what I am referring to as a *filling* and *fullness*, you may want to call *emptying* and *emptiness*. There is no difference because as we empty we find the truth of what is. These are seem-ingly opposite words that, for our purposes, mean the same thing. You must empty your small self to fill with the Divine.

> *Once you feel some vitality filling the area of the first chakra, move on to the second. Breathe in again through the root chakra, and this time draw the breath up to the area just above the perineum, the region just in front of the sacrum. As you breathe in, you now have two points, one directly above the other, along the line of the energetic spine that you are tracing. Be sure this line is vertical. You may want to adjust your posture at this point to correct some habitual leaning or tilting. Click yourself onto the vertical as you inhale. Do the same procedure with your exhalation as you did at the first chakra. Fill the region with life-force (or clear the region of everything). Continue in this way all through the chakras. Adjust your posture and align with the vertical at each step of the way. Don't move on to the next chakra until you can feel*

or imagine the one you are filling as full (or the one you are emptying as empty), lit up, or in some way cleansed by your conscious attention to it. If you find your mind to be very busy, you can chant the sacred syllable Om out loud on each out-breath. Let it help you fill each chakra with light. If when you set your Y-axis intention you chose a divine quality, you can use this word to breathe into each chakra. Love, beauty, wisdom. All good words to bring into your energetic matrix.

Once you have filled the entire Y-axis with breath, chant "Ah" out loud. "Ah" forms a vertical sound in the mouth and resonates well with Y-axis vibration. As you vocalize a prolonged "Ah" in the space of your newly cleansed and aligned energetic spine, you bring all your efforts in the individual chakras together as a unified whole. Imagine this sound homogeneously filling the vertical column of light at the core of your body. The sound "Ah" also vibrates at the core of the English word, "God".

⁊ This completes the ninth session. ⁊

This practice session corresponds to chapter

16

Practice Section

Session 10

Alignment for Healing

The first jhe building alignment exercise is an extension of the meditation you did in the last session. Bring the breath up through the root chakra to each consecutive chakra. The difference is that this time, when you breathe out, you will send the breath out along the X-axis of that chakra. Do this for 5 breaths. One for each body. That means that one complete cycle will include 35 breaths. On the in breath, silently sound Om. On the out breath, silently or out loud, speak a word that affirms a divine quality such as love, beauty, peace, joy, or harmony. For the sake of this example, I will use the word peace.

Here it is mapped out for you:

Root Chakra:

- ⇧ Breathe in through the root chakra. Silent Om.
- ⇔ Breathe out to the X-axis of the root chakra within the physical body. Peace.

⇑   Breathe in through the root chakra. Silent Om.
⇔   Breathe out to the X-axis of the root chakra through the etheric body. Peace.

⇑   Breathe in through the root chakra. Silent Om.
⇔   Breathe out to the X-axis of the root chakra through the astral body. Peace.

⇑   Breathe in through the root chakra. Silent Om.
⇔   Breathe out to the X-axis of the root chakra through the lower mental body. Peace.

⇑   Breathe in through the root chakra. Silent Om.
⇔   Breathe out to the X-axis of the root chakra through the higher mental body. Peace.

○ Second Chakra:
⇑   Breathe in through the root chakra and up to the second chakra. Silent Om.
⇔   Breathe out to the X-axis of the second chakra within the physical body. Peace.

⇑   Breathe in through the root chakra and up to the second chakra. Silent Om.
⇔   Breathe out to the X-axis of the second chakra through the etheric body. Peace.

⇑   Breathe in through the root chakra and up to the second chakra. Silent Om.
⇔   Breathe out to the X-axis of the second chakra through the astral body. Peace.

⇧ Breathe in through the root chakra and up to the second chakra. Silent Om.

⇔ Breathe out to the X-axis of the second chakra through the lower mental body. Peace.

⇧ Breathe in through the root chakra and up to the second chakra. Silent Om.

⇔ Breathe out to the X-axis of the second chakra through the higher mental body. Peace.

Continue on like this, breathing in through the root chakra, up through the energetic spine, and out to the X-axis of each chakra.

Shelves

Let's look at these nine landmarks again from bottom to top.

1. Pelvic floor
2. Sacral base
3. Diaphragm
4. Shoulders
5. Jaw
6. Mouth
7. Base of nose
8. Eyes
9. Eyebrows

The meditation is simple and powerful. Breathe naturally, softly. Let each breath come in and go out on its own. Then, just above the root chakra, in line with the pelvic floor, see this level's X-axis as it extends outward parallel to the horizon.

Moving up to the sacral base, see the next X-axis. Sense its position as parallel to the first and feel the field of peace that is beginning to hum in your lower torso. The next X-axis, at the diaphragm, links the upper and lower aspects of the physical field and it is the shelf that holds up the upper body. Feel it click into its parallel alignment with the others. The horizontal echo at the shoulders is also very powerful and your awareness of its presence may bring with it a heightened sense of peace as silence. We have a tendency to be highly identified with the face, so as we move into the region of the face, these X-axes take on a more personal intimacy. This is introduced gently with the horizontal suggestion of the jaw. It moves quickly and intensely into the very intimate region of the mouth.

- *As you align with the X-axis suggested by the line of the mouth, you add a strong voluntary energy to this process. This heightens the intentionality of the alignment.*
- *Aligning the base of the nose creates stillness.*
- *Aligning the horizontal of the eyes creates depth.*
- *Aligning at the level of the eyebrows generates spiritual surrender and a sense of reverence.*

See and feel all these parallel lines as they reveal their perfect relationships with each other. They distribute the weight like bookshelves. They allow space around all your structures so that they can function freely.

ᘒ This completes the tenth session. ᘒ.

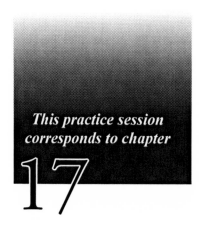

This practice session corresponds to chapter

17

The Z-axis is like a candy store. It is the major preoccupation of our culture. Our typical approach to manifestation of all the desires of the material world and relationships takes on catch phrases like *fame and fortune, money and power, sex, drugs, and rock and roll,* and so on. Usually we go grabbing after these things, feeling unfulfilled without them and then feeling unfulfilled once we get them. Usually we go after them with unaligned action first. Then we try to fix what we've done with more unaligned action.

Now, let's begin aligning the Z-axis for joyful manifestation. That means we dance toward our desires (and our desires themselves may transform as we refine our alignment), feeling joyful before they manifest and feeling joyful after they have manifested. What a big difference.

We do this in many ways. Here, in these exercises, we are laying the vibrational groundwork for joyful manifestation. In these exercises we will not be contemplating real estate or visualizing our perfect mate. Here we are simply aligning ourselves with our own inner Z-axis. This opens the path for inspired ideas. Those ideas lead to fruitful action. Those fruits become satisfying manifestation.

Alignment with Breath

Follow the same pattern as in aligning the X-axis. Rising through each chakra with the breath and extending the exhalation along the Z–axis of each chakra, broaden your awareness sequentially through the bodies.

For example:

⇧ Breathe in through the root chakra.
⤳ Exhale to fill the area of the physical body surrounding the chakra

⇧ Breathe in through the root chakra.
⤳ Exhale into the Z-axis of the chakra extending forward to the etheric body.

⇧ Breathe in through the root chakra.
⤳ Exhale into the Z-axis of the chakra extending forward to the astral body.

⇧ Breathe in through the root chakra.
⤳ Exhale into the Z-axis of the chakra extending forward to the lower mental body.

⇧ Breathe in through the root chakra.
⤳ Exhale into the Z-axis of the chakra extending forward to the higher mental body.

⇧ Breathe in through the root chakra.
⤳ Exhale into the Z-axis of the chakra extending forward merging into the Infinite.

Do the same for the second chakra, then the third, etc.

Variations

1. See the breath as light.
2. Chant the seed syllable for each chakra and send the sound out along the Z-axis to prepave the journey ahead of you regarding the attributes of the chakra.
3. Choose a divine quality that you want to reveal in your unfolding and impregnate your Z-axis on each breath with *love* or *peace* or *wisdom*.

 ♥ This completes the eleventh session. ♥

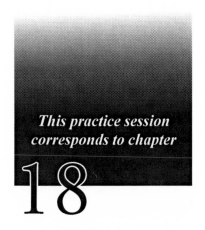

This practice session corresponds to chapter

T o integrate everything we have learned and have been practicing, we will distill it all down to one simple practice that can be done on a daily basis or whenever you want to quickly bring yourself into alignment. This does not replace all the other exercises but it is a handy encapsulation that I have found to be extremely useful.

Use this in the morning to align yourself for the day or at night for restorative sleep. Use it before going for an audition or competing in an athletic event. Use it before you ask your boss for a raise or before you ask your beloved to marry you. Use it before you head into rush hour traffic or before cleaning your house. Use it before you meditate or pray. It is yours. Find all the different moments in your life when you would benefit from heightened inner alignment and experiment with this. It is particularly useful before activities that involve the voice such as singing, public speaking, or to heighten authenticity in intimate conversation.

Chanting

In this process we will be using three sounds.

Ahh – corresponding to the Y-axis

Eee – Corresponding to the X-axis

Ooo – Corresponding to the Z-xis

If you look at the shape your mouth makes in order to produce these sounds, you will see these axes represented. Ah rises, Ee extends sideways, and Oo projects forward.

Spend a minute or so playing with these sounds in your mouth and get a sense of the direction of movement of each sound's energy. Exaggerate the movements of your mouth and lips as you fully express the vibrational message of these three sounds.

Now, we will revisit our alignment exercises with a new focus.

Breathe up through the root chakra.

On each exhalation, chant through a cycle of Ah-Ee-Oo. You may even want to extend the tail of the exhalation to reverberate between Ee-Oo-Ee-Oo several times.

> *With the Ah, align the root chakra with the Y-axis. With the Ee align the root chakra's X-axis. With the Oo align the root chakra's Z-axis.*

See the perfect right angles forming and vibrating with the sounds. I often move my hands in front of me to gesture the line of movement with each sound.

Continue tracing the energetic spine, aligning each chakra in this way. Check all your right angles as you go. You are revealing these axes in your consciousness, not imposing them. If you find a distortion, one side seems higher than the other, or your axis seems to twist, do not try to straighten it. Understand that it is a wave in your mind that is creating the illusion of a bend in your axis. If you are standing in a swimming pool and move the water with your hands, then look at your feet, they will appear to be all wiggly and bent. This is reflecting a disturbance in the medium through which you are perceiving.

The same is true for your axes. If you perceive something other than right angles between your axes, look deeper for the true axis that sits silently underneath your agitated perception. Rather than working to change the apparent axis, instead place your efforts toward quieting the waves of your mind so that you can perceive the true axis as it lives in you in perfect relationship with gravity and the natural axes of the three dimensional world which is your home.

Overtone Chanting

As you oscillate between the Ee and the Oo you may begin to hear overtones. These are resonant frequencies, making themselves audible, announcing the power of your inner alignment. This will further augment your alignment. Don't worry if you don't hear them. In time you probably will. They sound like harmonies sung by an invisible choir or flute. To encourage their audibility, chant your Ah as one pure sound coming from your root. Then, changing only the shape of your mouth and throat, let the same Ah, on the same breath, evolve into Ee and Oo as one smooth movement. You may hear a sequence of the following intervals over your voice: major 3rd, perfect 5th, minor 7th, octave. If you hear them, feel the added dimension of alignment they bring. They may be too faint for others to discern but if you hear them, enjoy!

⁓ This completes the twelfth session. ⁓

Audio versions of the Practice Section exercises are available at www.RootedintheInfinite.com.

Index

Register

Register your copy of **Rooted in the Infinite**

and receive additional lessons, audio, and updates.

Go to:

www.RootedintheInfinite.com

Enter the access information:

username: jhe

password: flow

Before you go...

This book explains the basics of the Yoga of Alignment (YOFA™) system. You can carry your practice further and deepen your results by extending your YOFA™ Training to include Affirmative Contemplation. Affirmative Contemplation bridges the gap between meditation and affirmation. You can use words, phrases, and even longer passages from sacred texts or other great writings to intensify your inner alignment practice.

Once you have begun your YOFA™ Training with the exercises in the Practice Section of this book, steep your awareness in the concentrated vibratory hum of words that ring true to the alignment you seek.

Affirmations, like desires, will usually hug one axis or another. You can craft affirmations for each axis. Always keep them in the present tense and stated in the positive. Then, as you close your inner alignment meditation sessions, float your Y-axis affirmations of divine love, inner peace, and connection to Source, vertically. Extend your X-axis healing affirmations out to the right and left. Roll out the red carpet before you with your Z-axis affirmations, prepaving your joyful manifestation, and preparing yourself to receive your heart's desire.

For more information about the Affirmative Contemplation process and for the YOFA™ *I Am Love* Affirmative Contemplation recordings, please visit www.AffirmativeContemplation.com

Printed in the United States
201139BV00003B/187-237/A

9 780978 906504